The Ultimate **5-Ingredient**

Diabetic Cookbook

1000-Day Simple and Healthy Recipes with 21 Days Meal Plan for Balanced Meals and Healthy Living

Virginia Renda

CONTENTS

Introduction

In a world driven mad by fear of unknown ailments such as cancers, diseases, and mental strain, being aware of and in control of your health is essential. Knowing whether you are a candidate for developing diabetes or already have it is vital to living a long, healthy, and fulfilling life.

As the maxim goes, knowledge is power, and this book is filled with all the knowledge I have acquired in my personal journey with diabetes. I share it here with the hope that you, too, can steer your life back onto the road of health and vitality.

I am going to be telling you some raw facts about diabetes, but I'm not a doctor, so I don't want to bore you with medical stuff. Instead, I am speaking from my heart, and from my own meandering experience. I am going to guide you through discovering your diabetes status, knowing the types of diabetes and what that means for you, explain some treatment options for diabetes, and help you reformulate your concepts around food, health, nutrition, and living wholeheartedly with diabetes.

It's not all easy. After all, we know the holidays are built around feasting and indulgences. So, how do you manage diabetes when everyone around you is living like it's their last hour? Even here, I have some solid advice to share, and you don't have to become the party pooper you fear you need to be when living with diabetes.

In the end, this book is about eating your way to better diabetic health, and once I have explained my foundation, I will bless you with amazing recipes based around the five-ingredient principle. You may ask why you should use five ingredients to prepare your diabetic meal plan. Simply put—it's easy. Focusing on less ingredients will ensure that you can easily balance your carbs, know your intake of carbs, and you will find flavors are fuller and more enhanced by the spices and prep you put in.

With fewer ingredients, it is easier to ensure you get a full spectrum of veggies, proteins, and healthy carbs. Additionally, you will find it much easier to prep these meals, shopping will become simpler, and you will feel an intense health benefit from the first bite.

Feeling inspired to manage your diabetic health better? Grab your spoon, and let's start cooking!

Chapter 1. Starting Your Diabetic Diet Journey

Types of Diabetes

Just as the causes of diabetes greatly vary, its types also vary, and each type is treated and controlled differently. If the cause is insulin resistance, you can not treat it by injecting more insulin. For that, you would need some other measures. So it is essential to know which type of diabetes you are suffering from. Here are the three types of diabetes:

1. Type I:

This type of diabetes is the result of the body's own autoimmune response. It means that our defense mechanism damages the pancreatic cells that produce insulin. As a result, our pancreas stops producing insulin or start producing them in an insufficient amount. This type of diabetes can happen at any time of your age, irrespective of your gender and the gene type. People suffering from diabetes type I need insulin to be injected artificially on day to day basis in order to maintain levels of glucose in their blood. They also can take insulin orally, but that it is usually not as effective as the direct injections.

2. Type II:

90% of diabetic patients suffer from this type of diabetes. It is mostly diagnosed in people of adults ages, but today, young adults are also equally susceptible to the disease. This type of diabetes can stay undetected for several years as it can only be identified through special tests. Good diet and constant exercise can only control the harms of this diabetes. The patient may require some extra dose of insulin both orally or through injections. It is also known as the 'Prediabetes,' and it is caused due to the inability of the body to respond to the insulin production in the body. There is no apparent damage to the cells producing the insulin unlike type I diabetes.

3. Gestational Diabetes (GDM)

As the name indicates it, this type of diabetes can occur to a mother during the gestational period or pregnancy. The good news is that it is not permanent but a temporary condition and persists only during the pregnancy. It is caused by the production of certain hormones from the placenta of the baby, and these hormones can disrupt the functioning of the insulin. So the body becomes insulin resistant. It is not always harmful, but the condition can get critical in case of malnutrition or poor dietary intake.

Ease the Effects of Diabetes by Eating a Healthy Meal

Eating healthy meals and doing a physical activity not only control the effect of diabetes, they can create a positive impact on overall health. To manage the effects of diabetes, you need to balance what you drink and eat with being active and taking diabetic medicines. Moreover, what you choose to eat, how much you eat and when you eat are all important in keeping your blood glucose level in check.

Indeed, making changes in your eating and drinking habits is challenging in the beginning, but once your body gets habitual with your new lifestyle, you can achieve your health goal in no time.

So being a person with diabetes doesn't mean that eating those foods that you don't enjoy. Not at all. The good news is that you can eat everything you love, but you have to consume small portions and less often. You can do this with the plate method. This method adds a variety of food in your plate and helps you control your portion sizes. For example, you can divide a plate into three portions, half of the plate for non-starchy veggies, the one-fourth portion for protein and the other one-fourth portion for grains, along with some fruits and a glass of low-fat milk.

Food to eat

The food you can eat in diabetes are:

- Vegetables: Some starchy vegetables including potatoes, peas, and corn
  All non-starchy vegetables such as bell peppers, tomatoes, broccoli, cauliflower, carrots, and leafy greens
- Fruits: All fruits that have low glycemic index including apples, bananas, berries, melon, grapes, oranges and avocado
- Grains: Wheat, rice, quinoa, barley, oats, cereal, cornmeal, whole wheat flour, pasta, tortillas
- Protein: Poultry such as chicken, turkey, and lamb, lean meat, meat substitutes such as tofu and tempeh, seafood, salmon, tuna and other fishes, eggs and dairy products such as low-fat milk, yogurt, and cheeses
- Nuts: Walnuts, peanuts, etc.
- Dried beans: Red beans, black beans, chickpeas, and split peas
- Oils: All oils that are liquid at room temperature, such as olive oil and canola oil
- Beverages: Unsweetened tea and coffee, plenty of water and a moderate amount of alcohol

Food to avoid

The foods and drinks that need to limit in diabetes are:

- Vegetables: All starchy vegetables except for those mentioned above.
- Fruits: All fruits that have a high glycemic index
- Protein: All high-fat dairy products
- White sugar
- Fried foods
- Foods that are high in salt, trans fats, and saturated fats
- Sweets such as candy, ice cream, and baked goods
- Processed foods and snacks
- Beverages that are sweetened such as processed juices, soda, and energy drink

The Plate Method

This is a very easy way to control what you eat. Firstly, start with a 9-inch plate. You should measure it to be sure about the size. Remember, the bigger your plate, the more you'll dish up, and the more you'll put into your body. So, 9 inches, no more.

The plate method is a popular theory that helps with weight loss, weight management, and calorie control. Each meal is served according to the following size guides:

- ½ plate of non-starchy vegetables (any veggie with fewer than 5 grams of carbs per serving)
- ¼ plate healthy protein (animal or plant-based is fine)
- ¼ high fiber carbs (no more than 15 grams for women or 30 grams for men)

You can also add some healthy fats but no more than 5-6 spoonfuls as part of a salad dressing, nuts or seeds, or in the meal prep for your food. Additionally, you may also notice that your plate is usually not full. This may sound crazy. But you should fill your plate, especially the ½ plate of non-starchy veggies. Most of us don't eat enough veggies and we don't consume nearly enough fiber. Don't forget to add your small cup of dairy such as yogurt or fruit to your daily intake too.

How to Prevent and Control Diabetes

If you have been diagnosed with Type-2 diabetes, you can prevent or delay diabetes. You should need to stay healthy and eat healthy foods. Therefore, lifestyle changes may lower diabetes. You feel better and strong than before.

1. Develop Good Habits

Type-2 diabetes may be lower by following healthy diets if you develop good habits such as lifestyle, healthy foods, regular exercise, medication, etc. It would be best to quit drinking such alcohol smoking because it may lead you towards managing active metabolic activities that may help you lower the risk of diabetes and live a healthy and good lifestyle.

2. Cut Refined Carbohydrates and Sugar from the Diet

You should quit these foods may help lower the risk of Type-2 diabetes. For example, foods high in carbohydrates and sugar increase blood sugar and insulin levels which may lead to hypoglycemia. The human body quickly breakdown the sugar and carbohydrate into small pieces that the brain absorbs. It may cause high blood sugar. Replace sugar food with low carb food may control diabetes. People who eat high sugary and high carbohydrate food quickly have Type-2 diabetes.

3. Drink a Lot of Water

Drinking a lot of water is best for those who have Type-2 diabetes. Drinking a lot of water lowers the risk of diabetes; this may increase blood sugar levels. Researcher shows that drinking water helps the body make the best insulin and control blood sugar. Water reduces the craving for sweets and salty drinks, which may help control blood sugar.

4. Quit Smoking

Smoking is related to an increased risk of diabetes, especially heavy smoking. Smoking may cause serious illnesses such as indigestion, prostate cancer, breast cancer, lung cancer, emphysema, heart diseases, etc. Quitting smoking may cause the risk of diabetes.

5. Drink Tea and Coffee

Studies show that including tea and coffee in your diet may help prevent diabetes. Researcher shows that intake of coffee daily reduces the risk of Type-2 diabetes. Coffee and tea consist of polyphenols and antioxidants, which may help prevent diabetes. Moreover, green tea has antioxidants, and it is also called epigallocatechin gallate, which has been recognized to lower the release of blood sugar from the liver.

6. Minimized Processed Food

Processed food is unhealthy for your health. You should minimize processed food. Cutting back on your diet and focusing on a healthy diet may help lower the risk of Type-2 diabetes. Improve your health to cut back on processed food in your diet. It causes health problems such as obesity, diabetes, heart diseases, etc. Intake of whole grain and supplements may help lower the risk of diabetes. Eat healthy fruits, vegetables, and whole grains.

7. Eat High Fiber Foods

Eating high fiber meals in every meal may help lower the risk of diabetes by preventing insulin and high blood sugar levels. Eating high fibers helps with weight management and stomach health. The fiber is divided into two types: soluble and insoluble. Soluble fiber dissolves in the water, but insoluble fiber does not dissolve in water.

8. Intake of Vitamin D

Eating food rich in vitamin D may help lower the risk of diabetes and improve vitamin D levels. Vitamin D is essential for controlling diabetes. Researcher shows that not getting vitamin D or having low blood pressure may cause Type-2 diabetes.

9. Regular Exercise

Daily physical activities such as walking and exercising help your brain break down the fats and sugars in the human blood by digesting food and releasing insulin from the pancreas. Moreover, exercise increases insulin in the brain. High-intensity exercise and aerobic exercise may help obese people lower blood sugar and control Type-2 diabetes. Regular exercise increases insulin secretion, which helps prevent Type-2 diabetes and lower blood sugar.

Chapter 2. Breakfast Recipes

Sweet Onion Frittata With Ham

Servings: 4
Cooking Time:8 Minutes
Ingredients:

- 4 ounces extra-lean, low-sodium ham slices, chopped
- 1 cup thinly sliced Vidalia onion
- 1 1/2 cups egg substitute
- 1/3 cup shredded, reduced-fat, sharp cheddar cheese

Directions:

1. Place a medium nonstick skillet over medium-high heat until hot. Coat the skillet with nonstick cooking spray, add ham, and cook until beginning to lightly brown, about 2–3 minutes, stirring frequently. Remove from skillet and set aside on separate plate.
2. Reduce the heat to medium, coat the skillet with nonstick cooking spray, add onions, and cook 4 minutes or until beginning to turn golden, stirring frequently.
3. Reduce the heat to medium low, add ham to the onions, and cook 1 minute (this allows the flavors to blend and the skillet to cool slightly before the eggs are added). Pour egg substitute evenly over all, cover, and cook 8 minutes or until puffy and set.
4. Remove the skillet from the heat, sprinkle cheese evenly over all, cover, and let stand 3 minutes to melt the cheese and develop flavors.

Nutrition Info:

- 110 cal., 2g fat (1g sag. fat), 20mg chol, 460mg sod., 6g carb (4g sugars, 0g fiber), 17g pro.

Fruity Cereal Bars

Servings: 20
Cooking Time: 30 Minutes
Ingredients:

- 3 tablespoons butter
- 1 package (10 ounces) large marshmallows
- 6 cups crisp rice cereal
- 1/2 cup chopped dried apple
- 1/2 cup dried cranberries

Directions:

1. In a large saucepan, combine butter and marshmallows. Cook and stir over medium-low heat until melted. Remove from the heat; stir in the cereal, apples and cranberries.
2. Pat into a 13-in. x 9-in. pan coated with cooking spray; cool. Cut into squares.

Nutrition Info:

- 105 cal., 2 g fat (1 g sat. fat), 5 mg chol., 102 mg sodium, 22 g carb., trace fiber, 1 g pro.

Honey Wheat Breadsticks

Servings: 16
Cooking Time: 40 Minutes
Ingredients:

- 1 1/3 cups water (70° to 80°)
- 3 tablespoons honey
- 2 tablespoons canola oil
- 1 1/2 teaspoons salt
- 2 cups bread flour
- 2 cups whole wheat flour
- 3 teaspoons active dry yeast

Directions:
1. In bread machine pan, place all ingredients in order suggested by manufacturer. Select dough setting (check dough after 5 minutes of mixing; add 1 to 2 tablespoons of water or flour if needed.
2. When cycle is completed, turn dough onto a lightly floured surface. Divide into 16 portions; shape each into a ball. Roll each into an 8-in. rope. Place 2 in. apart on greased baking sheets.
3. Cover and let rise in a warm place until doubled, about 30 minutes. Bake at 375° for 10-12 minutes or until golden brown. Remove to wire racks.

Nutrition Info:
- 131 cal., 2 g fat (trace sat. fat), 0 chol., 222 mg sodium, 25 g carb., 2 g fiber, 4 g pro.

Spinach And Feta Omelets

Servings:2
Cooking Time:10 Minutes
Ingredients:
- 4 large eggs
- 1 tablespoon canola oil
- 1 shallot, minced
- 4 ounces (4 cups) baby spinach
- 1 ounce feta cheese, crumbled (¼ cup)

Directions:
1. Beat 2 eggs with fork in bowl until eggs are thoroughly combined and color is pure yellow; do not overbeat. Repeat with remaining 2 eggs in second bowl.
2. Heat 1 teaspoon oil in 10-inch nonstick skillet over medium heat until shimmering. Add shallot and cook until softened, about 2 minutes. Stir in spinach and cook until wilted, about 1 minute. Using tongs, squeeze out any excess moisture from spinach mixture, then transfer to bowl and cover to keep warm. Wipe skillet clean with paper towels and let cool slightly.
3. Heat 1 teaspoon oil in now-empty skillet over medium heat until shimmering. Add 1 bowl of eggs and cook until edges begin to set, 2 to 3 seconds. Using rubber spatula, stir eggs in circular motion until slightly thickened, about 10 seconds. Use spatula to pull cooked edges of eggs in toward center, then tilt skillet to 1 side so that uncooked eggs run to edge of skillet. Repeat until omelet is just set but still moist on surface, 20 to 25 seconds. Sprinkle 2 tablespoons feta and half of spinach mixture across center of omelet.
4. Off heat, use spatula to fold lower third (portion nearest you) of omelet over filling; press gently with spatula to secure seam, maintaining fold. Run spatula between outer edge of omelet and skillet to loosen. Pull skillet sharply toward you few times to slide unfolded edge of omelet up far side of skillet. Jerk skillet again so that unfolded edge folds over itself, or use spatula to fold edge over. Invert omelet onto plate. Tidy edges with spatula and serve immediately.
5. Wipe skillet clean with paper towels and repeat with remaining 1 teaspoon oil, remaining eggs, remaining 2 tablespoons feta, and remaining filling.

Nutrition Info:
- 270 cal., 20g fat (6g sag. fat), 385mg chol, 320mg sod., 6g carb (2g sugars, 2g fiber), 16g pro.

Morning Cinnamon Rolls

Servings: 8
Cooking Time: 25 Minutes
Ingredients:

- 1 tube (8 ounces) refrigerated reduced-fat crescent rolls
- 1/2 teaspoon ground cinnamon
- Sugar substitute equivalent to 1/2 cup sugar, divided
- 1/4 cup confectioners' sugar
- 1 tablespoon fat-free milk

Directions:

1. Unroll crescent dough into a rectangle; seal seams and perforations. Combine the cinnamon and half of the sugar substitute; sprinkle over dough. Roll up jelly-roll style, starting with a long side; seal edge. Cut into eight slices.
2. Place rolls cut side down in a 9-in. round baking pan coated with cooking spray. Bake at 375° for 12-15 minutes or until golden brown.
3. In a small bowl, combine the confectioners' sugar, milk and remaining sugar substitute; drizzle over warm rolls.
4. TO FREEZE Cool unfrosted rolls and wrap in foil. Freeze for up to 3 months.
5. TO USE FROZEN ROLLS Thaw at room temperature; warm if desired. Follow directions for icing.

Nutrition Info:

- 123 cal., 5 g fat (1 g sat. fat), trace chol., 234 mg sodium, 18 g carb., trace fiber, 2 g pro.

Quick Veggie Frittata

Servings: 4
Cooking Time: 20 Minutes
Ingredients:

- 4 whole eggs
- 6 egg whites
- ¾ teaspoon Italian seasoning
- ¼ teaspoon salt
- Dash pepper
- 2 teaspoons canola or olive oil
- 2 cups frozen Italian-blend vegetables, thawed (from 1-lb bag)
- 2 tablespoons shredded Parmesan cheese

Directions:

1. In medium bowl, beat whole eggs, egg whites, Italian seasoning, salt and pepper until well mixed.
2. In 10-inch skillet, heat oil over medium heat. Pour egg mixture into skillet; top with vegetables. Reduce heat to medium-low. Cook 3 to 4 minutes, lifting eggs with spatula to allow uncooked portion to flow to bottom.
3. Cover; cook 7 to 8 minutes longer or until eggs are almost set but top is slightly moist. Top with cheese. Cover; cook 1 to 2 minutes or until cheese is melted.

Nutrition Info:

- 150 cal., 9g fat (2.5g sat. fat), 215 chol., 360mg sod., 4g carb. (2g sugars, 1g fiber), 14g pro.

Scrambled Eggs With Herbs

Servings:2
Cooking Time:x
Ingredients:
- 4 large eggs
- 2 teaspoons 1 percent low-fat milk
- Pinch salt
- Pinch pepper
- 1 teaspoon extra-virgin oil
- 2 tablespoons minced fresh chives, basil, and tarragon

Directions:

1. Beat eggs, milk, salt, and pepper with fork in bowl until eggs are thoroughly combined and color is pure yellow; do not overbeat.

2. Heat oil in 10-inch nonstick skillet over medium-high heat until shimmering, swirling to coat pan. Add egg mixture and, using rubber spatula, constantly and firmly scrape along bottom and sides of skillet until eggs begin to clump and spatula just leaves trail on bottom of pan, 45 to 75 seconds. Reduce heat to low and gently but constantly fold eggs until clumped and just slightly wet, 30 to 60 seconds. Quickly fold in herbs, then immediately transfer eggs to individual warmed plates. Serve immediately.

Nutrition Info:
- 170 cal., 12g fat (3g sag. fat), 370mg chol, 220mg sod., 1g carb (1g sugars, 0g fiber), 13g pro.

Good Morning Power Parfait

Servings: 4
Cooking Time: 5 Minutes
Ingredients:
- 1 ripe medium banana
- 2 cups fat-free, artificially sweetened, vanilla-flavored yogurt (divided use)
- 1 teaspoon ground cinnamon
- 1 cup whole strawberries, sliced
- 1/2 cup grape-nut-style cereal, preferably with raisins and almonds

Directions:

1. Add the banana, 1 cup yogurt, and 1 teaspoon cinnamon, if desired, to a blender and blend until smooth. Pour into 4 wine or parfait glasses.

2. Top each parfait with 1/4 cup sliced strawberries, 1/4 cup yogurt, and 2 tablespoons cereal.

Nutrition Info:
- 140 cal., 0g fat (0g sag. fat), 0mg chol, 125mg sod., 32g carb (14g sugars, 3g fiber), 5g pro.

Cheesy Mushroom Omelet

Servings: 2
Cooking Time:6 Minutes
Ingredients:
- 6 ounces sliced mushrooms
- 1/8 teaspoon black pepper
- 1/3 cup finely chopped green onion (green and white parts)
- 1 cup egg substitute
- 2 tablespoons crumbled bleu cheese (about 1/4 cup) or 1/4 cup shredded, reduced-fat, sharp cheddar cheese

Directions:
1. Place a small skillet over medium-high heat until hot. Coat with nonstick cooking spray and add mushrooms and pepper. Coat the mushrooms with nonstick cooking spray and cook 4 minutes or until soft, stirring frequently.
2. Add the onions and cook 1 minute longer. Set the pan aside.
3. Place another small skillet over medium heat until hot. Coat with nonstick cooking spray and add the egg substitute. Cook 1 minute without stirring. Using a rubber spatula, lift up the edges to allow the uncooked portion to run under. Cook 1–2 minutes longer or until eggs are almost set and beginning to puff up slightly.
4. Spoon the mushroom mixture on one half of the omelet, sprinkle the cheese evenly over the mushrooms, and gently fold over. Cut in half to serve.

Nutrition Info:
- 110 cal., 2g fat (1g sag. fat), 5mg chol, 340mg sod., 6g carb (3g sugars, 1g fiber), 16g pro.

Orange-honey Yogurt

Servings:1
Cooking Time:7 Minutes
Ingredients:
- 1 cup 2 percent Greek yogurt
- 2 tablespoons honey
- ¼ teaspoon grated orange zest plus 2 tablespoons juice

Directions:
1. Whisk ingredients together in bowl. (Yogurt can be refrigerated for up to 3 days.) Serve.

Nutrition Info:
- 15 cal., 0g fat (0g sag. fat), 0mg chol, 0mg sod., 2g carb (2g sugars, 0g fiber), 1g pro.

Sausage Potato Skillet Casserole

Servings: 4
Cooking Time:17 Minutes
Ingredients:
- 5 ounces reduced-fat, smoked turkey sausage, kielbasa style
- 2 cups chopped onion
- 4 cups frozen hash brown potatoes with peppers and onions
- 1/3 cup shredded, reduced-fat, sharp cheddar cheese

Directions:
1. Cut the sausage in fourths lengthwise. Cut each piece of sausage in 1/4-inch pieces.
2. Place a large nonstick skillet over medium-high heat until hot. Coat the skillet with nonstick cooking spray, add sausage, and cook 3 minutes or until the sausage begins to brown, stirring frequently. Set the sausage aside on a separate plate.
3. Recoat the skillet with nonstick cooking spray, add the onions, and cook 5 minutes or until the onions begin to brown, stirring frequently.
4. Reduce the heat to medium, add the frozen potatoes and sausage, and cook 9 minutes or until the potatoes are lightly browned, stirring occasionally.
5. Remove the skillet from the heat, top with cheese, cover, and let stand 5 minutes to melt the cheese and develop flavors.

Nutrition Info:
- 190 cal., 5g fat (2g sag. fat), 25mg chol, 450mg sod., 26g carb (5g sugars, 4g fiber), 9g pro.

Blackberry Smoothies

Servings:4
Cooking Time: 10 Minutes
Ingredients:
- 1 cup orange juice
- 1 cup (8 ounces) plain yogurt
- 2 to 3 tablespoons honey
- 1 1/2 cups fresh or frozen blackberries
- 1/2 cup frozen unsweetened mixed berries
- Additional blackberries and yogurt, optional

Directions:
1. In a blender, combine the first five ingredients; cover and process for about 15 seconds or until smooth. Pour into chilled glasses; serve immediately. If desired top with additional blackberries and yogurt.

Nutrition Info:
- 130 cal., 2g fat (1g sat. fat), 8mg chol., 29mg sod., 26g carb. (21g sugars, 3g fiber), 3g pro.

Double-duty Banana Pancakes

Servings: 8
Cooking Time:6 Minutes
Ingredients:
- 2 ripe medium bananas, thinly sliced
- 1 cup buckwheat pancake mix
- 3/4 cup plus 2 tablespoons fat-free milk
- 4 tablespoons light pancake syrup

Directions:
1.   Mash one half of the banana slices and place in a medium bowl with the pancake mix and the milk. Stir until just blended.
2.   Place a large nonstick skillet over medium heat until hot. (To test, sprinkle with a few drops of water. If the water drops "dance" or jump in the pan, it's hot enough.) Coat the skillet with nonstick cooking spray, add two scant 1/4 cup measures of batter, and cook the pancakes until puffed and dry around the edges, about 1 minute.
3.   Flip the pancakes and cook until golden on the bottom. Place on a plate and cover to keep warm.
4.   Recoat the skillet with nonstick cooking spray, add three scant 1/4 cup measures of batter, and cook as directed. Repeat with the remaining batter.
5.   Place 2 pancakes on each of 4 dinner plates, top with equal amounts of banana slices, and drizzle evenly with the syrup. If you like, place the dinner plates in a warm oven and add the pancakes as they are cooked.

Nutrition Info:
- 100 cal., 0g fat (0g sag. fat), 0mg chol, 140mg sod., 23g carb (9g sugars, 2g fiber), 3g pro.

Yogurt Parfaits

Servings:4
Cooking Time:8 Minutes
Ingredients:
- 1 cup whole almonds, toasted and chopped
- ½ cup raw sunflower seeds, toasted
- 3 cups low-fat plain yogurt
- 20 ounces (4 cups) blackberries, blueberries, raspberries, and/or sliced strawberries

Directions:
1.   Combine almonds and sunflower seeds in bowl. Using four 16-ounce glasses, spoon ¼ cup yogurt into each glass, then top with ⅓ cup berries, followed by 2 tablespoons nut mixture. Repeat layering process 2 more times with remaining yogurt, berries, and nut mixture. Serve.

Nutrition Info:
- 480 cal., 29g fat (4g sag. fat), 10mg chol, 130mg sod., 39g carb (24g sugars, 11g fiber), 22g pro.

Breakfast Grilled Swiss Cheese And Rye

Servings: 2
Cooking Time:7 Minutes
Ingredients:
- 2 slices rye bread
- 4 teaspoons reduced-fat margarine (35% vegetable oil)
- 2 large eggs
- 1 1/2 ounces sliced, reduced-fat Swiss cheese, torn in small pieces

Directions:
1. Spread one side of each bread slice with 1 teaspoon margarine and set aside.
2. Place a medium skillet over medium heat until hot. Coat with nonstick cooking spray and add the egg substitute. Cook 1 minute without stirring. Using a rubber spatula, lift up the edges to allow the uncooked portion to run under. Cook 1–2 minutes longer or until eggs are almost set and beginning to puff up slightly. Flip and cook 30 seconds.
3. Remove the skillet from the heat and spoon half of the eggs on the unbuttered sides of two of the bread slices. Arrange equal amounts of the cheese evenly over each piece.
4. Return the skillet to medium heat until hot. Coat the skillet with nonstick cooking spray. Add the two sandwiches and cook 3 minutes. If the cheese doesn't melt when frying the sandwich bottom, put it under the broiler until brown. Using a serrated knife, cut each sandwich in half.

Nutrition Info:
- 250 cal., 13g fat (4g sag. fat), 200mg chol, 360mg sod., 17g carb (2g sugars, 2g fiber), 16g pro.

Almond Quinoa With Cranberries

Servings: 4
Cooking Time:17 Minutes
Ingredients:
- 4 ounces slivered almonds
- 3/4 cup dry quinoa
- 3 tablespoons dried cranberries
- 1 tablespoon honey (or 1 tablespoon cinnamon sugar)

Directions:
1. Heat a large saucepan over medium-high heat. Add almonds and cook 2 minutes or until beginning to lightly brown, stirring frequently. Set aside on separate plate.
2. Pour 1 1/2 cups water into the saucepan and bring to a boil, add the quinoa, reduce heat to low, cover and cook 13–15 minutes or until liquid is absorbed. Remove from heat and let stand, covered, for 5 minutes.
3. Top with the almonds and cranberries. Drizzle with the honey (or sprinkle with cinnamon sugar.)

Nutrition Info:
- 330 cal., 16g fat (1g sag. fat), 0mg chol, 0mg sod., 39g carb (12g sugars, 6g fiber), 11g pro.

Busy Day Breakfast Burrito

Servings: 4
Cooking Time:3 Minutes
Ingredients:

- 1 1/2 cups egg substitute
- 4 (6-inch) whole-wheat flour tortillas
- 1/4 cup fresh, no-salt-added pico de gallo
- 1/2 cup shredded, reduced-fat, sharp cheddar cheese

Directions:

1. Place a small nonstick skillet over medium heat until hot. Coat the skillet with nonstick cooking spray, add egg substitute, and cook, without stirring, until egg mixture begins to set on bottom, about 1 minute.
2. Draw a spatula across the bottom of pan to form large curds. Continue cooking until egg mixture is thick but still moist; do not stir constantly.
3. Place the tortillas on a microwave-safe plate and microwave on HIGH for 15 seconds or until heated. Top each with equal amounts of the egg mixture.
4. Spoon 1 tablespoon pico de gallo evenly over the egg on each tortilla, sprinkle with 2 tablespoons cheese, and roll up.

Nutrition Info:

- 180 cal., 4g fat (2g sag. fat), 5mg chol, 450mg sod., 18g carb (2g sugars, 1g fiber), 16g pro.

English Muffin Melts

Servings: 8
Cooking Time:3 Minutes
Ingredients:

- 4 whole-wheat English muffins, cut in half
- 2 tablespoons reduced-fat mayonnaise
- 3 ounces sliced reduced-fat Swiss cheese, torn in small pieces
- 4 ounces oven-roasted deli turkey, finely chopped

Directions:

1. Preheat the broiler.
2. Arrange the muffin halves on a baking sheet and place under the broiler for 1–2 minutes or until lightly toasted. Remove from broiler and spread 3/4 teaspoon mayonnaise over each muffin half.
3. Arrange the cheese pieces evenly on each muffin half and top with the turkey.
4. Return to the broiler and cook 3 minutes, or until the turkey is just beginning to turn golden and the cheese has melted.

Nutrition Info:

- 120 cal., 3g fat (1g sag. fat), 15mg chol, 290mg sod., 15g carb (3g sugars, 2g fiber), 9g pro.

Strawberry-carrot Smoothies

Servings:5
Cooking Time: 5 Minutes
Ingredients:
- 2 cups (16 ounces) reduced-fat plain Greek yogurt
- 1 cup carrot juice
- 1 cup orange juice
- 1 cup frozen pineapple chunks
- 1 cup frozen unsweetened sliced strawberries

Directions:
1. Place all ingredients in a blender; cover and process until smooth.

Nutrition Info:
- 141 cal., 2g fat (1g sat. fat), 5mg chol., 79mg sod., 20g carb. (15g sugars, 1g fiber), 10g pro.

Popcorn With Olive Oil

Servings:14
Cooking Time:10 Minutes
Ingredients:
- 1 tablespoon water
- ½ cup popcorn kernels
- 2 tablespoons extra-virgin olive oil
- ½ teaspoon salt
- ½ teaspoon pepper

Directions:
1. Heat Dutch oven over medium-high heat for 2 minutes. Add water and popcorn, cover, and cook, shaking frequently, until first few kernels begin to pop. Continue to cook, shaking vigorously, until popping slows to about 2 seconds between pops. Transfer popcorn to large serving bowl and toss with oil, salt, and pepper. Serve.

Nutrition Info:
- 90 cal., 4g fat (0g sag. fat), 0mg chol, 170mg sod., 10g carb (0g sugars, 2g fiber), 1g pro.

Whole Wheat Buttermilk Rolls

Servings: 6
Cooking Time: 45 Minutes
Ingredients:
- 1 1/2 cups self-rising flour
- 1 1/2 cups whole wheat flour
- 1/3 cup sugar
- 1 package (1/4 ounce) quick-rise yeast
- 1 cup buttermilk
- 1/4 cup canola oil

Directions:
1. In a large bowl, combine the self-rising flour, 3/4 cup whole wheat flour, sugar and yeast. In a small saucepan, heat buttermilk and oil to 120°-130° (mixture will appear curdled). Add to dry ingredients; beat just until smooth. Stir in remaining whole wheat flour.
2. Turn onto a lightly floured surface; knead until smooth and elastic, about 6-8 minutes. Cover and let dough rest for 10 minutes.
3. Roll dough to 1/2-in. thickness; cut with a floured 2 1/2-in. biscuit cutter. Place 2 in. apart on baking sheets coated with cooking spray. Cover and let rise in a warm place until doubled, about 35-40 minutes.
4. Bake at 375° for 8-12 minutes or until golden brown. Serve warm.

Nutrition Info:
- 116 cal., 3 g fat (trace sat. fat), 1 mg chol., 135 mg sodium, 19 g carb., 1 g fiber, 3 g pro.

Kale Chips

Servings:8
Cooking Time:60 Minutes
Ingredients:
- 12 ounces Lacinato kale, stemmed and torn into 3-inch pieces
- 1 tablespoon extra-virgin olive oil
- ½ teaspoon kosher salt

Directions:
1. Adjust oven racks to upper-middle and lower-middle positions and heat oven to 200 degrees. Set wire racks in 2 rimmed baking sheets. Dry kale thoroughly between dish towels, transfer to large bowl, and toss with oil and salt.
2. Arrange kale on prepared racks, making sure leaves overlap as little as possible. Bake kale until very crisp, 45 to 60 minutes, switching and rotating sheets halfway through baking. Let kale chips cool completely before serving. (Kale chips can be stored in paper towel–lined airtight container for up to 1 day.)

Nutrition Info:
- 60 cal., 4g fat (0g sag. fat), 0mg chol, 160mg sod., 5g carb (1g sugars, 2g fiber), 3g pro.

Peach Cranberry Quick Bread

Servings: 14
Cooking Time:45 Minutes
Ingredients:
- 1 (15.6-ounce) box cranberry quick bread and muffin mix
- 1 cup water
- 1/2 cup egg substitute or 4 large egg whites
- 2 tablespoons canola oil
- 2 cups chopped frozen and thawed unsweetened peaches

Directions:
1. Preheat the oven to 375°F.
2. Coat a nonstick 9 × 5-inch loaf pan with nonstick cooking spray.
3. Beat the bread mix, water, egg substitute, and oil in a medium bowl for 50 strokes or until well blended. Stir in the peaches and spoon into the loaf pan. Bake 45 minutes or until a wooden toothpick comes out clean.
4. Place the loaf pan on a wire rack for 20 minutes before removing the bread from the pan. Cool completely for peak flavor and texture.

Nutrition Info:
- 150 cal., 3g fat (0g sag. fat), 0mg chol, 150mg sod., 29g carb (15g sugars, 1g fiber), 3g pro.

Raisin French Toast With Apricot Spread

Servings: 4
Cooking Time:6 Minutes Per Batch
Ingredients:
- 8 slices whole-wheat cinnamon raisin bread
- 3 tablespoons no-trans-fat margarine (35% vegetable oil)
- 1/4 cup apricot or any flavor all-fruit spread
- 1 cup egg substitute (divided use)

Directions:
1. Arrange 4 bread slices on the bottom of a 13 × 9-inch baking pan. Pour 1/2 cup egg substitute evenly over all and turn several times to coat. Let stand 2 minutes to absorb egg slightly.
2. Meanwhile, using a fork, stir the margarine and fruit spread together in a small bowl until well blended.
3. Place a large nonstick skillet over medium heat until hot. Liberally coat the skillet with nonstick cooking spray, add 4 bread slices (leaving any remaining egg mixture in the baking pan), and cook 3 minutes.
4. Turn and cook 3 minutes longer or until the bread is golden brown. For darker toast, turn the slices again and cook 1 minute more. Set aside on a serving platter and cover to keep warm.
5. While the first batch is cooking, place the remaining bread slices in the baking pan and pour the remaining egg substitute evenly over all. Turn several times to coat. Cook as directed.
6. Serve each piece of toast topped with 1 tablespoon of the margarine mixture.

Nutrition Info:
- 260 cal., 6g fat (1g sag. fat), 0mg chol, 390mg sod., 37g carb (17g sugars, 4g fiber), 12g pro.

Chapter 3. Appetizers And Snacks

Tropical Treats

Servings: 4
Cooking Time: 5 Minutes
Ingredients:

- 2 cups (16 ounces) reduced-fat plain yogurt
- 1 can (8 ounces) unsweetened crushed pineapple, drained
- 2 teaspoons sugar
- 1/4 teaspoon coconut extract
- 1/4 teaspoon grated lime peel

Directions:

1. In a small bowl, combine all ingredients. Chill until serving.

Nutrition Info:

- 121 cal., 2 g fat (1 g sat. fat), 7 mg chol., 86 mg sodium, 20 g carb., trace fiber, 7 g pro.

Mocha Pumpkin Seeds

Servings:3
Cooking Time: 25 Minutes
Ingredients:

- 6 tablespoons sugar
- 2 tablespoons baking cocoa
- 1 tablespoon instant coffee granules
- 1 large egg white
- 2 cups salted shelled pumpkin seeds (pepitas)

Directions:

1. Preheat oven to 325°. Place sugar, cocoa and coffee granules in a small food processor; cover and pulse until finely ground.
2. In a bowl, whisk egg white until frothy. Stir in pumpkin seeds. Sprinkle with sugar mixture; toss to coat evenly. Spread in a single layer in a parchment paper-lined 15x10x1-in. baking pan.
3. Bake 20-25 minutes or until dry and no longer sticky, stirring seeds every 10 minutes. Cool completely in pan. Store in an airtight container.

Nutrition Info:

- 142 cal., 10g fat (2g sat. fat), 0 chol., 55mg sod., 10g carb. (7g sugars, 1g fiber), 6g pro.

Basil Spread And Water Crackers

Servings: 4
Cooking Time: 5 Minutes
Ingredients:
- 2 ounces reduced-fat garlic and herb cream cheese
- 1/2 cup finely chopped fresh basil
- 12 fat-free water crackers

Directions:
1. Stir the cream cheese and basil together in a small bowl until well blended.
2. Place 1 teaspoon spread on each cracker.

Nutrition Info:
- 70 cal., 2g fat (1g sag. fat), 0mg chol, 200mg sod., 9g carb (1g sugars, 0g fiber), 3g pro.

Crostini With Kalamata Tomato

Servings: 4
Cooking Time:10 Minutes
Ingredients:
- 4 ounces multigrain baguette bread, cut in 12 slices (about 1/4 inch thick)
- 1 small tomato, finely chopped
- 9 small kalamata olives, pitted and finely chopped
- 2 tablespoons chopped fresh basil

Directions:
1. Preheat the oven to 350°F.
2. Arrange the bread slices on a baking sheet and bake 10 minutes or until just golden on the edges. Remove from the heat and cool completely.
3. Meanwhile, stir the remaining ingredients together in a small bowl. Spread 1 tablespoon of the mixture on each bread slice.

Nutrition Info:
- 90 cal., 2g fat (0g sag. fat), 0mg chol, 220mg sod., 16g carb (2g sugars, 1g fiber), 3g pro.

Sparkling Party Punch

Servings: 5
Cooking Time: 17 Minutes
Ingredients:
- 1 can (46 ounces) unsweetened pineapple juice, chilled
- 3 cups apricot nectar or juice, chilled
- 1 liter diet lemon-lime soda, chilled
- Pineapple sherbet, optional

Directions:
1. In a punch bowl, combine the pineapple juice, apricot nectar and soda. Top with scoops of sherbet if desired. Serve immediately.
Nutrition Info:
- 66 cal., trace fat (trace sat. fat), 0 chol., 9 mg sodium, 16 g carb., trace fiber, trace pro.

Tortellini Appetizers

Servings: 6
Cooking Time: 25 Minutes
Ingredients:
- 18 refrigerated cheese tortellini
- 1/4 cup fat-free Italian salad dressing
- 6 thin slices (4 ounces) reduced-fat provolone cheese
- 6 thin slices (2 ounces) Genoa salami
- 18 large pimiento-stuffed olives

Directions:
1. Cook tortellini according to package directions; drain and rinse in cold water. In a resealable plastic bag, combine tortellini and salad dressing. Seal bag and refrigerate for 4 hours.
2. Place a slice of cheese on each slice of salami; roll up tightly. Cut into thirds. Drain tortellini and discard dressing. For each appetizer, thread a tortellini, salami roll-up and olive on a toothpick.

Nutrition Info:
- 92 cal., 6 g fat (3 g sat. fat), 16 mg chol., 453 mg sodium, 5 g carb., trace fiber, 7 g pro.

Zippy Tortilla Chips

Servings: 2
Cooking Time: 20 Minutes
Ingredients:
- 1/2 teaspoon brown sugar
- 1/4 teaspoon garlic powder
- 1/4 teaspoon onion powder
- 1/4 teaspoon ground cumin
- 1/4 teaspoon paprika
- 1/8 teaspoon cayenne pepper
- 4 corn tortillas (6 inches)
- Cooking spray

Directions:
1. In a small bowl, combine the first six ingredients. Stack the tortillas; cut into six wedges. Arrange in a single layer on a baking sheet coated with cooking spray.
2. Spritz the wedges with cooking spray; sprinkle with seasoning mixture. Bake at 375° for 9-10 minutes or until lightly browned. Cool for 5 minutes.

Nutrition Info:
- 138 cal., 3 g fat (trace sat. fat), 0 chol., 85 mg sodium, 26 g carb., 3 g fiber, 3 g pro.

Banana Mocha Cooler

Servings: 3
Cooking Time: 5 Minutes
Ingredients:

- 1 cup low-fat vanilla frozen yogurt
- 3/4 cup fat-free milk
- 1 medium ripe banana, sliced
- 1 teaspoon instant coffee granules
- 1 cup ice cubes (7 to 8)

Directions:

1. In a blender, combine all ingredients. Cover and process for 45-60 seconds or until frothy. Pour into glasses; serve immediately.

Nutrition Info:

- 122 cal., 1 g fat (1 g sat. fat), 5 mg chol., 72 mg sodium, 24 g carb., 1 g fiber, 6 g pro.

Strawberry Tofu Smoothies

Servings: 2
Cooking Time: 10 Minutes
Ingredients:

- 1 cup unsweetened apple juice
- 1 1/2 cups frozen unsweetened strawberries
- 4 ounces silken firm tofu, cubed
- 1 teaspoon sugar

Directions:

1. In a blender, combine all ingredients; cover and process for 45-60 seconds or until smooth. Pour into chilled glasses; serve immediately.

Nutrition Info:

- 136 cal., 2 g fat (trace sat. fat), 0 chol., 25 mg sodium, 26 g carb., 3 g fiber, 5 g pro.

Lime'd Blueberries

Servings: 6
Cooking Time: 5 Minutes
Ingredients:

- 2 cups frozen unsweetened blueberries, partially thawed
- 1/4 cup frozen grape juice concentrate
- 1 1/2 tablespoons lime juice

Directions:

1. Place all ingredients in a medium bowl and toss gently.
2. Serve immediately for peak flavor and texture.

Nutrition Info:

- 50 cal., 0g fat (0g sag. fat), 0mg chol, 5mg sod., 13g carb (11g sugars, 1g fiber), 0g pro.

Tomato-jalapeno Granita

Servings:6
Cooking Time: 15 Minutes
Ingredients:
- 2 cups tomato juice
- 1/3 cup sugar
- 4 mint sprigs
- 1 jalapeno pepper, sliced
- 2 tablespoons lime juice
- Fresh mint leaves, optional

Directions:
1. In a small saucepan, bring the tomato juice, sugar, mint sprigs and jalapeno to a boil. Cook and stir until sugar is dissolved. Remove from the heat; cover and let stand 15 minutes.
2. Strain and discard solids. Stir in lime juice. Transfer to a 1-qt. dish; cool to room temperature. Freeze for 1 hour; stir with a fork.
3. Freeze 2-3 hours longer or until completely frozen, stirring every 30 minutes. Scrape granita with a fork just before serving; spoon into dessert dishes. If desired garnish with additional mint leaves.

Nutrition Info:
- 59 cal., 0 fat (0 sat. fat), 0 chol., 205mg sod., 15g carb. (13g sugars, 0 fiber), 1g pro.

Savory Apple-chicken Sausage

Servings: 8
Cooking Time: 25 Minutes
Ingredients:
- 1 large tart apple, peeled and diced
- 2 teaspoons poultry seasoning
- 1 teaspoon salt
- 1/4 teaspoon pepper
- 1 pound ground chicken

Directions:
1. In a large bowl, combine the apple, poultry seasoning, salt and pepper. Crumble chicken over mixture and mix well. Shape into eight 3-in. patties.
2. In a large skillet coated with cooking spray, cook patties over medium heat for 5-6 minutes on each side or until no longer pink.

Nutrition Info:
- 92 cal., 5 g fat (1 g sat. fat), 38 mg chol., 328 mg sodium, 4 g carb., 1 g fiber, 9 g pro.

Spiced Coffee

Servings: 2
Cooking Time: 20 Minutes
Ingredients:

- 2 cups water
- 5 teaspoons instant coffee granules
- 1/2 cinnamon stick (3 inches)
- 4 whole cloves
- 5 teaspoons sugar
- Whipped topping, optional

Directions:

1. In a small saucepan, combine the water, coffee granules, cinnamon stick and cloves. Bring to a boil. Remove from the heat; cover and let stand for 5-8 minutes. Strain and discard spices. Stir in sugar until dissolved. Ladle into mugs. Serve with whipped topping if desired.

Nutrition Info:

- 46 cal., trace fat (trace sat. fat), 0 chol., 1 mg sodium, 11 g carb., 0 fiber, trace pro.

Turkey Reubens

Servings: 4
Cooking Time: 25 Minutes
Ingredients:

- 8 slices rye bread
- 1/2 pound thinly sliced deli turkey
- 1/2 cup sauerkraut, rinsed and well drained
- 4 slices reduced-fat Swiss cheese
- 1/4 cup fat-free Thousand Island salad dressing

Directions:

1. On four slices of bread, layer the turkey, sauerkraut, cheese and salad dressing. Top with remaining bread. Spritz both sides of sandwiches with butter-flavored cooking spray.
2. In a large nonstick skillet over medium heat, toast sandwiches on both sides until cheese is melted.

Nutrition Info:

- 310 cal., 8 g fat (3 g sat. fat), 35 mg chol., 1,398 mg sodium, 39 g carb., 5 g fiber, 22 g pro.

Sweet Peanut Buttery Dip

Servings: 4
Cooking Time: 5 Minutes
Ingredients:

- 1/3 cup fat-free vanilla-flavored yogurt
- 2 tablespoons reduced-fat peanut butter
- 2 teaspoons packed dark brown sugar
- 2 medium bananas, sliced

Directions:

1. Using a fork or whisk, stir the yogurt, peanut butter, and brown sugar together in a small bowl until completely blended.
2. Serve with banana slices and wooden toothpicks, if desired.

Nutrition Info:

- 120 cal., 3g fat (0g sag. fat), 0mg chol, 40mg sod., 21g carb (12g sugars, 2g fiber), 3g pro.

Baby Carrots And Spicy Cream Dip

Servings: 4
Cooking Time: 5 Minutes
Ingredients:
- 1/3 cup fat-free sour cream
- 3 tablespoons reduced-fat tub-style cream cheese
- 3/4 teaspoon hot pepper sauce
- 1/8 teaspoon salt
- 48 baby carrots

Directions:
1. Stir the sour cream, cream cheese, pepper sauce, and salt together until well blended.
2. Let stand at least 10 minutes to develop flavors and mellow slightly. Serve with carrots.

Nutrition Info:
- 90 cal., 2g fat (1g sag. fat), 10mg chol, 240mg sod., 16g carb (7g sugars, 3g fiber), 3g pro.

Raspberry-banana-yogurt Smoothies

Servings: 3
Cooking Time: 10 Minutes
Ingredients:
- 1 container (6 oz) French vanilla low-fat yogurt
- 1½ cups original-flavored soymilk
- 1 cup frozen or fresh unsweetened raspberries
- 1 medium banana, sliced (1 cup)

Directions:
1. In blender or food processor, place all ingredients. Cover; blend on high speed about 30 seconds or until smooth.
2. Pour into 3 glasses. Serve immediately.
3. Strawberry-Banana-Yogurt Smoothies: Use strawberry yogurt in place of the vanilla yogurt and fresh or frozen strawberries in place of the raspberries.

Nutrition Info:
- 190 cal., 3g fat (1g sat. fat), 5 chol., 115mg sod., 33g carb. (21g sugars, 6g fiber), 7g pro.

Bird's Nest Breakfast Cups

Servings: 6
Cooking Time: 30 Minutes
Ingredients:
- 12 turkey bacon strips
- 1 1/2 cups egg substitute
- 6 tablespoons shredded reduced-fat Mexican cheese blend
- 1 tablespoon minced fresh parsley

Directions:
1. In a large skillet, cook bacon over medium heat for 2 minutes on each side or until partially set but not crisp. Coat six muffin cups with cooking spray; wrap two bacon strips around the inside of each cup. Fill each with 1/4 cup egg substitute; top with cheese.
2. Bake at 350° for 18-20 minutes or until set. Cool for 5 minutes before removing from pan. Sprinkle with the parsley.

Nutrition Info:
- 120 cal., 7 g fat (2 g sat. fat), 30 mg chol., 515 mg sodium, 2 g carb., trace fiber, 12 g pro.

Fruit Smoothies

Servings: 4
Cooking Time: 10 Minutes
Ingredients:
- 2 cups 2% milk
- 1 cup frozen unsweetened sliced peaches
- 1 cup frozen unsweetened strawberries
- 1/4 cup orange juice
- 2 tablespoons honey

Directions:
1. In a blender, combine all ingredients. Cover and process until smooth. Pour into chilled glasses; serve immediately.

Nutrition Info:
- 128 cal., 2 g fat (1 g sat. fat), 9 mg chol., 62 mg sodium, 23 g carb., 1 g fiber, 5 g pro.

Strawberry Breakfast Shortcakes

Servings: 2
Cooking Time: 10 Minutes
Ingredients:

- 4 frozen low-fat multigrain waffles
- 1 cup fresh strawberries, sliced
- 1/2 cup plain Greek yogurt
- Maple syrup

Directions:

1. Prepare waffles according to package directions. Divide among two serving plates. Top with strawberries and yogurt. Serve with syrup.

Nutrition Info:

- 230 cal., 8 g fat (4 g sat. fat), 15 mg chol., 466 mg sodium, 36 g carb., 4 g fiber, 7 g pro.

Parmesan–black Pepper Breadsticks

Servings: 12
Cooking Time: 30 Minutes
Ingredients:

- 2 cups Bisquick Heart Smart® mix
- ½ cup plus 1 tablespoon cold water
- ½ teaspoon cracked black pepper
- 5 tablespoons shredded Parmesan cheese (about 1¼ oz)
- Olive oil cooking spray
- Additional cracked black pepper, if desired

Directions:

1. Heat oven to 400°F. Line cookie sheet with parchment paper to prevent sticking. In medium bowl, stir together Bisquick mix, water, ½ teaspoon pepper and 2 tablespoons of the cheese until soft dough forms.
2. Sprinkle work surface with additional baking mix. Place dough on surface; roll to coat. With rolling pin, roll into 10 × 8-inch rectangle. Spray top of dough with cooking spray. Sprinkle with remaining 3 tablespoons cheese; press in gently. Starting on 10-inch side, cut crosswise into 12 (8-inch) strips. Gently twist each strip. Place ½ inch apart on cookie sheet. Sprinkle with additional pepper.
3. Bake 10 to 12 minutes until light golden brown. Serve warm.

Nutrition Info:

- 90 cal., 2.5g fat (0.5g sat. fat), 0 chol., 260mg sod., 14g carb. (2g sugars, 0g fiber), 3g pro.

Creamy Peaches

Servings: 4
Cooking Time: 10 Minutes
Ingredients:

- 1 can (15 ounces) sliced peaches in extra-light syrup, drained
- 1 1/2 cups (12 ounces) fat-free cottage cheese
- 4 ounces fat-free cream cheese, cubed
- Sugar substitute equivalent to 1 tablespoon sugar

Directions:
1. Thinly slice four peach slices; set aside for garnish. Place remaining peaches in a food processor; add the cottage cheese. Cover and process until blended. Add cream cheese and sugar substitute; cover and process until blended.
2. Spoon into four serving dishes. Top with reserved peaches. Refrigerate until serving.

Nutrition Info:
- 127 cal., trace fat (trace sat. fat), 6 mg chol., 443 mg sodium, 15 g carb., 1 g fiber, 15 g pro.

Apple Breakfast Wedges

Servings: 4
Cooking Time: 10 Minutes
Ingredients:

- 2 medium apples
- 1 cup Rice Chex, crushed
- 1 1/2 teaspoons packed brown sugar
- 2 tablespoons reduced-fat creamy peanut butter

Directions:
1. Core apples; cut each into six wedges. Pat dry with paper towels.
2. In a small shallow bowl, combine the cereal and brown sugar. Spread cut sides of apples with peanut butter; roll in cereal mixture. Serve immediately.

Nutrition Info:
- 36 cal., 1 g fat (trace sat. fat), 0 chol., 33 mg sodium, 6 g carb., 1 g fiber, 1 g pro.

Grilled Shrimp With Spicy-sweet Sauce

Servings: 15
Cooking Time: 30 Minutes
Ingredients:
- 3 tablespoons reduced-fat mayonnaise
- 2 tablespoons sweet chili sauce
- 1 green onion, thinly sliced
- 3/4 teaspoon Sriracha Asian hot chili sauce or 1/2 teaspoon hot pepper sauce
- 45 uncooked large shrimp (about 1 1/2 pounds), peeled and deveined
- 1/4 teaspoon salt
- 1/4 teaspoon pepper

Directions:
1. In a small bowl, mix mayonnaise, chili sauce, green onion and Sriracha. Sprinkle shrimp with salt and pepper. Thread three shrimp onto each of the 15 metal or soaked wooden skewers.
2. Moisten a paper towel with cooking oil; using long-handled tongs, rub on grill rack to coat lightly. Grill shrimp, covered, over medium heat or broil 4 in. from heat 3-4 minutes on each side or until the shrimp turn pink. Serve with the sauce.

Nutrition Info:
- 56 cal., 2 g fat (trace sat. fat), 61 mg chol., 156 mg sodium, 2 g carb., trace fiber, 8 g pro.

Sweet Pineapple Cider

Servings: 12
Cooking Time: 30 Minutes
Ingredients:
- 2 small apples, divided
- 10 whole cloves
- 1 bottle (48 ounces) unsweetened apple juice
- 4 cans (6 ounces each) unsweetened pineapple juice
- 2 cinnamon sticks (3 inches)

Directions:
1. Core and cut one apple into 10 slices. Insert one clove into each slice. In a Dutch oven, combine juices. Add apple slices and cinnamon sticks. Bring to a boil. Reduce heat; simmer, uncovered, for 15-20 minutes or until flavors are blended.
2. Discard apple slices and cinnamon sticks. Core and cut remaining apple into 12 slices. Ladle cider into mugs; garnish with apple slices. Serve warm.

Nutrition Info:
- 93 cal., trace fat (trace sat. fat), 0 chol., 5 mg sodium, 23 g carb., trace fiber, trace pro.

Asparagus Ham Roll-ups

Servings: 16
Cooking Time: 25 Minutes
Ingredients:

- 16 fresh asparagus spears, trimmed
- 1 medium sweet red pepper, cut into 16 strips
- 8 ounces Havarti cheese, cut into 16 strips
- 8 thin slices deli ham or prosciutto, cut in half lengthwise
- 16 whole chives

Directions:

1. In a large skillet, bring 1 in. of water to a boil. Add asparagus; cover and cook for 3 minutes. Drain and immediately place asparagus in ice water. Drain and pat dry.
2. Place an asparagus spear, red pepper strip and cheese strip on each piece of ham. Roll up tightly; tie with a chive. Refrigerate until serving.

Nutrition Info:

- 69 cal., 5 g fat (3 g sat. fat), 18 mg chol., 180 mg sodium, 2 g carb., trace fiber, 6 g pro.

Goat Cheese Crostini

Servings: 16
Cooking Time: 10 Minutes
Ingredients:

- 1 cup crumbled goat cheese
- 1 teaspoon minced fresh rosemary
- 1 French bread baguette (10 1/2 ounces), cut into 1/2-inch slices and toasted
- 3 tablespoons honey
- 1/4 cup slivered almonds, toasted

Directions:

1. In a small bowl, combine cheese and rosemary; spoon over toast slices. Drizzle with honey; sprinkle with almonds.
2. BACON-ALMOND CROSTINI Combine 2 cups shredded Monterey Jack cheese, 2/3 cup mayonnaise, 1/2 cup toasted sliced almonds, 6 slices crumbled cooked bacon, 1 chopped green onion and a dash of salt. Spread over toast. Bake for 5-7 minutes or until cheese is melted. Sprinkle with additional almonds if desired.

Nutrition Info:

- 76 cal., 4 g fat (2 g sat. fat), 6 mg chol., 92 mg sodium, 9 g carb., 1 g fiber, 3 g pro.

Sausage & Salsa Breakfast Burritos

Servings: 6
Cooking Time: 20 Minutes
Ingredients:

- 5 breakfast turkey sausage links
- 2 cartons (8 ounces each) egg substitute
- 1/2 cup salsa
- 1/4 teaspoon pepper
- 6 whole wheat tortilla (8 inches), warmed
- 1/2 cup shredded reduced-fat cheddar cheese

Directions:
1. Cook sausage links according to package directions. Meanwhile, in a large bowl, whisk the egg substitute, salsa and pepper. Pour into a large nonstick skillet coated with cooking spray. Cook and stir over medium heat until eggs are nearly set. Chop the sausage links. Add to egg mixture; cook and stir until completely set.
2. Spoon 1/3 cup egg mixture off center on each tortilla and sprinkle with 4 teaspoons cheese. Fold sides and ends over filling and roll up.

Nutrition Info:
- 265 cal., 10 g fat (3 g sat. fat), 25 mg chol., 602 mg sodium, 25 g carb., 2 g fiber, 18 g pro.

Bleu Cheese'd Pears

Servings: 4
Cooking Time: 5 Minutes
Ingredients:

- 2 ounces fat-free cream cheese
- 3 1/2 tablespoons crumbled bleu cheese
- 2 medium firm pears, halved, cored, and sliced into 20 slices

Directions:
1. In a small bowl, microwave the cheeses on HIGH for 10 seconds to soften. Use a rubber spatula to blend well.
2. Top each pear slice with 3/4 teaspoon cheese.
3. To prevent the pear slices from discoloring, toss them with a tablespoon of orange, pineapple, or lemon juice. Shake off the excess liquid before topping them with cheese.

Nutrition Info:
- 90 cal., 2g fat (1g sag. fat), 10mg chol, 190mg sod., 14g carb (9g sugars, 3g fiber), 4g pro.

Tuna Salad Stuffed Eggs

Servings: 4
Cooking Time:10 Minutes
Ingredients:
- 4 large eggs
- 1 (2.6-ounce) packet tuna (or 5-ounce can of tuna packed in water, rinsed and well drained)
- 2 tablespoons reduced-fat mayonnaise
- 1 1/2–2 tablespoons sweet pickle relish

Directions:
1. Place eggs in a medium saucepan and cover with cold water. Bring to a boil over high heat, then reduce the heat and simmer 10 minutes.
2. Meanwhile, stir the tuna, mayonnaise, and relish together in a small bowl.
3. When the eggs are cooked, remove them from the water and let stand one minute before peeling under cold running water. Cut eggs in half, lengthwise, and discard 4 egg yolk halves and place the other 2 egg yolk halves in the tuna mixture and stir with a rubber spatula until well blended. Spoon equal amounts of the tuna mixture in each of the egg halves.
4. Serve immediately, or cover with plastic wrap and refrigerate up to 24 hours.

Nutrition Info:
- 90 cal., 4g fat (1g sag. fat), 105mg chol, 240mg sod., 3g carb (2g sugars, 0g fiber), 9g pro.

Dilled Chex Toss

Servings: 18
Cooking Time:30 Minutes
Ingredients:
- 6 cups multi-grain or Wheat Chex cereal
- 4-ounce packet ranch salad dressing mix
- 1 tablespoon dried dill
- 2 tablespoons extra virgin olive oil

Directions:
1. Preheat the oven to 175°F.
2. Place the cereal, dressing mix, and dill in a large zippered plastic bag. Seal and shake gently to blend well.
3. Place the mixture on a large rimmed baking sheet or jelly roll pan, drizzle the oil evenly over all, and stir thoroughly to blend. Spread out in a single layer and bake 30 minutes or until browned lightly, stirring once.

Nutrition Info:
- 50 cal., 1g fat (0g sag. fat), 0mg chol, 200mg sod., 8g carb (1g sugars, 1g fiber), 1g pro.

Creamy Apricot Fruit Dip

Servings: 4
Cooking Time: 5 Minutes
Ingredients:
- 1/3 cup fat-free vanilla-flavored yogurt
- 1/4 cup fat-free whipped topping
- 2 tablespoons apricot all-fruit spread
- 2 cups whole strawberries or 2 medium apples, halved, cored, and sliced

Directions:
1. In a small bowl, whisk the yogurt, whipped topping, and fruit spread until well blended.
2. Serve with fruit.

Nutrition Info:
- 60 cal., 0g fat (0g sag. fat), 0mg chol, 15mg sod., 14g carb (9g sugars, 2g fiber), 1g pro.

Cucumber Punch

Servings: 25
Cooking Time: 15 Minutes
Ingredients:
- 2 medium cucumbers
- 3 cups water
- 1 can (12 ounces) frozen lemonade concentrate, thawed
- 2 liters diet ginger ale, chilled
- 4 1/2 cups diet grapefruit or citrus soda, chilled

Directions:
1. With a zester or fork, score cucumbers lengthwise; cut widthwise into thin slices. In a large pitcher, combine water and lemonade concentrate; add cucumbers. Cover and refrigerate overnight.
2. Just before serving, transfer cucumber mixture to a punch bowl; stir in ginger ale and grapefruit soda.

Nutrition Info:
- 29 cal., trace fat (trace sat. fat), 0 chol., 15 mg sodium, 7 g carb., trace fiber, trace pro.

Peppered Pork Pitas

Servings: 4
Cooking Time: 20 Minutes
Ingredients:
- 1 pound boneless pork loin chops, cut into thin strips
- 1 tablespoon olive oil
- 2 teaspoons coarsely ground pepper
- 2 garlic cloves, minced
- 1 jar (12 ounces) roasted sweet red peppers, drained and julienned
- 4 whole pita breads, warmed

Directions:
1. In a small bowl, combine the pork, oil, pepper and garlic; toss to coat. In a large skillet, saute pork mixture until no longer pink. Add red peppers; heat through. Serve with pita breads.
Nutrition Info:
- 380 cal., 11 g fat (3 g sat. fat), 55 mg chol., 665 mg sodium, 37 g carb., 2 g fiber, 27 g pro.

Minutesi Feta Pizzas

Servings:4
Cooking Time: 20 Minutes
Ingredients:

- 2 whole wheat English muffins, split and toasted
- 2 tablespoons reduced-fat cream cheese
- 4 teaspoons prepared pesto
- 1/2 cup thinly sliced red onion
- 1/4 cup crumbled feta cheese

Directions:

1. Preheat oven to 425°. Place muffins on a baking sheet.
2. Mix cream cheese and pesto; spread over muffins. Top with onion and feta cheese. Bake until lightly browned, 6-8 minutes.

Nutrition Info:

- 136 cal., 6g fat (3g sat. fat), 11mg chol., 294mg sod., 16g carb. (4g sugars, 3g fiber), 6g pro.

Raspberry Fizz

Servings: 1
Cooking Time: 5 Minutes
Ingredients:

- 2 ounces ruby red grapefruit juice
- 1/2 to 1 ounce raspberry flavoring syrup
- 1/2 to 3/4 cup ice cubes
- 6 ounces club soda, chilled

Directions:

1. In a mixing glass or tumbler, combine grapefruit juice and syrup. Place ice in a highball glass; add juice mixture. Top with club soda.

Nutrition Info:

- 70 cal., 0 fat (0 sat. fat), 0 chol., 37 mg sodium, 18 g carb., 0 fiber, trace pro.

Balsamic-goat Cheese Grilled Plums

Servings:8
Cooking Time: 25 Minutes
Ingredients:

- 1 cup balsamic vinegar
- 2 teaspoons grated lemon peel
- 4 medium firm plums, halved and pitted
- 1/2 cup crumbled goat cheese

Directions:

1. For glaze, in a small saucepan, combine vinegar and lemon peel; bring to a boil. Cook 10-12 minutes or until mixture is thickened and reduced to about 1/3 cup (do not overcook).
2. Grill plums, covered, over medium heat 2-3 minutes on each side or until tender. Drizzle with glaze; top with goat cheese.

Nutrition Info:

- 58 cal., 2g fat (1g sat. fat), 9mg chol., 41mg sod., 9g carb. (8g sugars, 1g fiber), 2g pro.

Raisin & Hummus Pita Wedges

Servings:8
Cooking Time: 15 Minutes
Ingredients:
- 1/4 cup golden raisins
- 1 tablespoon chopped dates
- 1/2 cup boiling water
- 2 whole wheat pita breads (6 inches)
- 2/3 cup hummus
- Snipped fresh dill or dill weed, optional

Directions:
1. Place raisins and dates in a small bowl. Cover with boiling water; let stand for 5 minutes. Drain well.
2. Cut each pita into four wedges. Spread with hummus; top with raisins, dates and, if desired, dill.

Nutrition Info:
- 91 cal., 2g fat (0 sat. fat), 0 chol., 156mg sod., 16g carb. (4g sugars, 3g fiber), 3g pro.

Potato Basil Scramble

Servings: 4
Cooking Time: 30 Minutes
Ingredients:
- 2 cups cubed potatoes
- 1/2 cup chopped onion
- 1/2 chopped green pepper
- 1 tablespoon vegetable oil
- 2 cups egg substitute
- 2 tablespoons minced fresh basil
- 1/2 teaspoon salt
- 1/8 teaspoon cayenne pepper

Directions:
1. Place potatoes in a microwave-safe bowl; add 1 in. of water. Cover and microwave on high for 7 minutes; drain.
2. In a large nonstick skillet coated with cooking spray, saute the onion, green pepper and potatoes in oil until tender. Add the egg substitute, basil, salt and pepper. Cook and stir over medium heat until the eggs are completely set.

Nutrition Info:
- 163 cal., 4 g fat (0.55 g sat. fat), 0 chol., 549 mg sodium, 19 g carb., 2 g fiber, 14 g pro.

Strawberry-watermelon-pomegranate Smoothies

Servings: 5
Cooking Time: 20 Minutes

Ingredients:

- 2 cups frozen whole strawberries
- 2 cups diced seeded watermelon
- 1 cup pomegranate or cranberry juice
- 2 containers (6 oz each) French vanilla low-fat yogurt
- 1 tablespoon honey

Directions:

1. In blender, place all ingredients.
2. Cover; blend on high speed about 30 seconds or until smooth. Serve immediately.

Nutrition Info:

- 160 cal., 1g fat (0.5g sat. fat), 0 chol., 50mg sod., 33g carb. (28g sugars, 2g fiber), 4g pro.

Creamy Cottage Cheese With Cucumbers

Servings: 5
Cooking Time: 15 Minutes

Ingredients:

- 2 cups 2% reduced-fat cottage cheese
- ¼ cup reduced-fat sour cream
- 3 tablespoons chopped fresh chives or green onions
- ½ teaspoon seasoned salt
- ¼ teaspoon lemon-pepper seasoning
- 3 medium cucumbers, cut into ¼-inch slices

Directions:

1. In medium bowl, mix all ingredients except cucumbers.
2. Serve dip with cucumber slices.

Nutrition Info:

- 120 cal., 3.5g fat (2g sat. fat), 10 chol., 530mg sod., 9g carb. (6g sugars, 1g fiber), 14g pro.

Blue Cheese-stuffed Strawberries

Servings: 8
Cooking Time: 25 Minutes

Ingredients:

- 1/2 cup balsamic vinegar
- 3 ounces fat-free cream cheese
- 2 ounces crumbled blue cheese
- 16 fresh strawberries
- 3 tablespoons finely chopped pecans, toasted

Directions:

1. Place vinegar in a small saucepan. Bring to a boil; cook until liquid is reduced by half. Cool to room temperature.
2. Meanwhile, in a small bowl, beat cream cheese until smooth. Beat in blue cheese. Remove stems and scoop out centers from strawberries; fill each with about 2 teaspoons cheese mixture. Sprinkle pecans over filling, pressing lightly. Chill until serving. Drizzle with balsamic vinegar.

Nutrition Info:

- 36 cal., 2 g fat (1 g sat. fat), 3 mg chol., 80 mg sodium, 3 g carb., trace fiber, 2 g pro.

Pineapple Iced Tea

Servings: 5
Cooking Time: 10 Minutes
Ingredients:
- 4 cups water
- 7 individual tea bags
- 1 cup unsweetened pineapple juice
- 1/3 cup lemon juice
- 2 tablespoons sugar

Directions:
1. In a large saucepan, bring water to a boil. Remove from the heat.
2. Add tea bags; cover and steep for 3-5 minutes. Discard tea bags. Stir in the pineapple juice, lemon juice and sugar until sugar is dissolved. Refrigerate overnight for the flavors to blend. Serve over ice.

Nutrition Info:
- 51 cal., 0 fat (0 sat. fat), 0 chol., 1 mg sodium, 13 g carb., 0 fiber, 0 pro.

Strawberry Orange Vinegar

Servings: 2
Cooking Time: 10 Minutes
Ingredients:
- 1 medium orange
- 2 cups white wine vinegar
- 2 tablespoons sugar
- 2 cups sliced fresh strawberries

Directions:
1. Using a citrus zester, peel rind from orange in long narrow strips (being careful not to remove pith). In a large saucepan, heat vinegar and sugar to just below the boiling point. Place strawberries in a warm sterilized quart jar; add heated vinegar mixture and orange peel. Cover and let stand in a cool dark place for 10 days.
2. Strain mixture through a cheesecloth; discard pulp and orange rind. Pour into a sterilized pint jar. Seal tightly. Store in the refrigerator for up to 6 months.

Nutrition Info:
- 15 cal., trace fat (trace sat. fat), 0 chol., trace sodium, 4 g carb., trace fiber, trace pro.

Chapter 4. Meat Recipes

Anytime Skillet Pork

Servings: 4
Cooking Time:10 Minutes
Ingredients:
- 4 thin pork chops with bone in, trimmed of fat (about 1 1/4 pounds total)
- 1/3 cup water
- 1 1/2 teaspoons Worcestershire sauce
- 1 1/2 teaspoons lite soy sauce

Directions:
1. Place a large nonstick skillet over medium-high heat until hot. Coat with nonstick cooking spray.
2. Liberally sprinkle the pork chops with pepper, if desired, and cook 3 minutes. Turn and cook 3 more minutes or until the pork is barely pink in the center. Set the pork aside on a separate plate and cover with foil to keep warm.
3. Stir the remaining ingredients together in a small bowl. Add the mixture to the skillet and bring to a boil over medium-high heat. Boil for 3–4 minutes or until the liquid is reduced to 2 tablespoons, stirring frequently. Spoon the sauce over the pork

Nutrition Info:
- 120 cal., 3g fat (1g sag. fat), 60mg chol, 150mg sod., 1g carb (0g sugars, 0g fiber), 22g pro.

Country-style Ham And Potato Casserole

Servings: 4
Cooking Time: 15 Minutes
Ingredients:
- 6 ounces lean smoked deli ham, (preferably Virginia ham), thinly sliced and chopped
- 1 pound red potatoes, scrubbed and thinly sliced
- 1 medium onion, thinly sliced
- 1/3 cup shredded, reduced-fat, sharp cheddar cheese

Directions:
1. Preheat the oven to 350°F.
2. Place a medium nonstick skillet over medium-high heat until hot. Coat the skillet with nonstick cooking spray, add ham, and cook 5 minutes or until the ham edges are beginning to lightly brown, stirring frequently. Remove from the heat and set the ham aside on a separate plate.
3. Layer half of the potatoes and half of the onions in the bottom of the skillet. Top with the ham and repeat with layers of potatoes and onions. Sprinkle with black pepper, if desired, and cover tightly with a sheet of foil.
4. Bake 35–40 minutes or until the potatoes are tender when pierced with a fork. Remove from the oven, top with cheese, and let stand, uncovered, for 3 minutes to melt the cheese and develop flavors.

Nutrition Info:
- 170 cal., 2g fat (1g sag. fat), 25mg chol, 420mg sod., 23g carb (4g sugars, 2g fiber), 13g pro.

Grapefruit-zested Pork

Servings: 4
Cooking Time:6 Minutes
Ingredients:

- 3 tablespoons lite soy sauce
- 1/2–1 teaspoon grapefruit zest
- 3 tablespoons grapefruit juice
- 1 jalapeño pepper, seeded and finely chopped, or 1/8–1/4 teaspoon dried red pepper flakes
- 4 thin lean pork chops with bone in (about 1 1/4 pounds total)

Directions:

1. Combine all ingredients in a large zippered plastic bag. Seal tightly and toss back and forth to coat evenly. Refrigerate overnight or at least 8 hours.
2. Preheat the broiler.
3. Coat the broiler rack and pan with nonstick cooking spray, arrange the pork chops on the rack (discarding the marinade), and broil 2 inches away from the heat source for 3 minutes. Turn and broil 3 minutes longer or until the pork is no longer pink in the center.

Nutrition Info:

- 130 cal., 3g fat (1g sag. fat), 60mg chol, 270mg sod., 2g carb (1g sugars, 0g fiber), 23g pro.

Cheesy Steak And Potato Skillet

Servings: 4
Cooking Time: 30 Minutes
Ingredients:

- 1 lb boneless beef sirloin steak, cut into 4 serving pieces
- ½ teaspoon garlic-pepper blend
- ¼ teaspoon seasoned salt
- 1 tablespoon canola oil
- 1½ cups frozen bell pepper and onion stir-fry (from 1-lb bag)
- 1 bag (1 lb 4 oz) refrigerated home-style potato slices
- ¾ cup shredded reduced-fat sharp Cheddar cheese (3 oz)

Directions:

1. Sprinkle beef pieces with ¼ teaspoon of the garlic-pepper blend and ⅛ teaspoon of the seasoned salt. In 12-inch nonstick skillet, cook beef over medium-high heat 3 to 4 minutes, turning once or twice, until brown and desired doneness. Remove from skillet; keep warm.
2. In same skillet, heat oil over medium heat. Add stir-fry vegetables; cook 2 minutes, stirring frequently. Add potatoes; sprinkle with remaining ¼ teaspoon garlic-pepper blend and ⅛ teaspoon seasoned salt. Cook uncovered 8 to 10 minutes, stirring frequently, until tender.
3. Place beef in skillet with potatoes, pushing potatoes around beef. Cook 1 to 2 minutes, turning beef once, until thoroughly heated. Sprinkle with cheese; cover and heat until cheese is melted.

Nutrition Info:

- 350 cal., 9g fat (2.5g sat. fat), 70 chol., 510mg sod., 33g carb. (3g sugars, 2g fiber), 34g pro.

Southwestern Protein-powered Bowls

Servings: 4
Cooking Time:15 Minutes
Ingredients:

* 3/4 pound 90% extra-lean ground beef
* 1 (12.7-ounce) package frozen vegetable and grain protein blends, southwestern variety, such as Birds Eye Steam Fresh
* 1 (14.5-ounce) can no-salt-added diced tomatoes
* 1 tablespoon ground cumin

Directions:

1. Heat a Dutch oven over medium-high heat. Add beef and cook until browned, stirring frequently. Stir in the frozen vegetable mixture, tomatoes, and 1 cup water. Bring to a boil. Reduce heat to medium-low, cover, and cook 10 minutes.
2. Remove from heat. Stir in the cumin, 1/4 teaspoon salt, and 1/4 teaspoon pepper, if desired.
3. Spoon equal amounts into 4 bowls.

Nutrition Info:

* 280 cal., 9g fat (3g sag. fat), 50mg chol, 450mg sod., 25g carb (4g sugars, 8g fiber), 23g pro.

Zesty Beef Patties With Grilled Onions

Servings: 4
Cooking Time:15 Minutes
Ingredients:

* 1 pound 96% lean ground beef
* 1 tablespoon Dijon mustard
* 4 teaspoons ranch-style salad dressing and seasoning mix (available in packets)
* 1 large yellow onion, thinly sliced
* 1/4 cup water

Directions:

1. Mix the ground beef, mustard, and salad dressing mix together in a medium bowl. Shape the beef mixture into 4 patties.
2. Place a large nonstick skillet over medium-high heat until hot. Coat the skillet with nonstick cooking spray and add the onions. Coat the onions with nonstick cooking spray and cook 7 minutes or until they are richly browned, stirring frequently. Set them aside on a separate plate.
3. Recoat the skillet with nonstick cooking spray, add the patties, and cook 4 minutes. Flip the patties and cook another 3 minutes or until they are no longer pink in the center. Place them on a serving platter.
4. Add the onions and water to the pan drippings and cook 30 seconds, scraping the bottom and sides of the skillet. When the mixture has thickened slightly, spoon it over the patties.

Nutrition Info:

* 190 cal., 5g fat (2g sag. fat), 65mg chol, 450mg sod., 8g carb (3g sugars, 1g fiber), 26g pro.

Steak Marsala

Servings: 4
Cooking Time: 20 Minutes
Ingredients:
- 4 beef tenderloin steaks, ¾ inch thick (about 1 lb)
- ½ teaspoon salt
- ¼ teaspoon pepper
- 2 cloves garlic, crushed
- 1 tablespoon drained capers
- ½ cup Marsala wine or nonalcoholic red wine

Directions:
1. Sprinkle both sides of each beef steak with salt and pepper. Rub with garlic. Spray 10-inch skillet with cooking spray; heat over medium-high heat. Add beef; cook 6 to 8 minutes, turning once, until desired doneness. Remove beef from skillet; cover to keep warm.
2. Add capers and wine to skillet. Heat to boiling over high heat. Cook uncovered 3 to 4 minutes, stirring frequently, until liquid is slightly reduced. Serve sauce over beef.

Nutrition Info:
- 190 cal., 8g fat (3g sat. fat), 50 chol., 390mg sod., 2g carb. (0g sugars, 0g fiber), 26g pro.

Prosciutto-pepper Pork Chops

Servings: 4
Cooking Time: 20 Minutes
Ingredients:
- 4 boneless pork loin chops (4 ounces each)
- 1/8 teaspoon garlic powder
- 1/8 teaspoon pepper
- 2 teaspoons canola oil
- 4 thin slices prosciutto or deli ham
- 1/2 cup julienned roasted sweet red peppers
- 2 slices reduced-fat provolone cheese, cut in half

Directions:
1. Sprinkle pork chops with garlic powder and pepper. In a large nonstick skillet, cook chops in oil over medium heat for 4-5 minutes on each side or until a thermometer reads 145°.
2. Top each pork chop with prosciutto, red peppers and cheese. Cover and cook for 1-2 minutes or until the cheese is melted. Let stand for 5 minutes before serving.

Nutrition Info:
- 237 cal., 12 g fat (4 g sat. fat), 72 mg chol., 483 mg sodium, 1 g carb., trace fiber, 28 g pro.

Spicy Chili'd Sirloin Steak

Servings: 4
Cooking Time:11 Minutes
Ingredients:

- 1 pound boneless sirloin steak, trimmed of fat
- 2 tablespoons chili seasoning (available in packets)
- 1/8 teaspoon salt

Directions:
1. Coat both sides of the sirloin with the chili seasoning mix, pressing down so the spices adhere. Let stand 15 minutes, or overnight in the refrigerator for a spicier flavor (let steak stand at room temperature 15 minutes before cooking).
2. Place a large nonstick skillet over medium-high heat until hot. Coat the skillet with nonstick cooking spray, add the beef, and cook 5 minutes. Turn the steak, reduce the heat to medium, cover tightly, and cook 5 minutes. Do not overcook. Remove the skillet from the heat and let stand 2 minutes, covered.
3. Sprinkle the steak with salt and cut into 1/4-inch slices. Pour any accumulated juices over the steak slices.

Nutrition Info:
- 140 cal., 4g fat (1g sag. fat), 40mg chol, 250mg sod., 2g carb (0g sugars, 0g fiber), 23g pro.

Black Bean And Beef Tostadas

Servings: 4
Cooking Time: 30 Minutes
Ingredients:

- 8 ounces lean ground beef (90% lean)
- 1 can (10 ounces) diced tomatoes and green chilies, undrained
- 1 can (15 ounces) black beans, rinsed and drained
- 1 can (16 ounces) refried beans
- 8 tostada shells
- Optional toppings: shredded lettuce, shredded reduced-fat Mexican cheese blend, sour cream and/or salsa

Directions:
1. In a large skillet, cook beef over medium heat until no longer pink; drain. Stir in tomatoes. Bring to a boil. Reduce heat; simmer, uncovered, for 6-8 minutes or until liquid is reduced to 2 tablespoons. Stir in black beans; heat through.
2. Spread refried beans over tostada shells. Top with beef mixture. Serve with toppings of your choice.

Nutrition Info:
- 390 cal., 11 g fat (3 g sat. fat), 44 mg chol., 944 mg sodium, 49 g carb., 12 g fiber, 24 g pro.

Christmas Carol Ham

Servings: 8
Cooking Time: 120 Minutes
Ingredients:

- 2 pounds fully cooked boneless ham, cut into eight slices
- 1/2 cup packed brown sugar
- 1/4 cup unsweetened pineapple juice
- 1 1/2 teaspoons white vinegar
- 1/4 teaspoon ground mustard

Directions:
1. Place ham slices in a 3-qt. slow cooker. In a small bowl, combine the brown sugar, pineapple juice, vinegar and mustard; pour over ham. Cover and cook on low for 2-3 hours or until heated through.
Nutrition Info:
- 186 cal., 5 g fat (2 g sat. fat), 83 mg chol., 1,237 mg sodium, 15 g carb., trace fiber, 21 g pro.

Maple Pork With Figs

Servings: 4
Cooking Time: 25 Minutes
Ingredients:

- 4 bone-in pork loin chops, ½ inch thick (about 1¼ lb), trimmed of fat
- ½ teaspoon salt
- ½ cup apple juice or dry red wine
- ¼ cup real maple syrup
- ⅓ cup coarsely chopped dried figs
- 1 teaspoon cornstarch
- ¼ cup water

Directions:

1. Spray 12-inch skillet with cooking spray; heat skillet over medium-high heat. Sprinkle pork with salt; place in skillet. Cook about 5 minutes, turning once, until browned. Remove from skillet; keep warm.
2. In same skillet, cook apple juice, maple syrup and figs over medium-high heat 5 minutes, stirring frequently.
3. In small bowl, mix cornstarch and water; stir into juice mixture. Cook over medium-high heat about 2 minutes, stirring constantly, until thickened and clear.
4. Reduce heat to medium. Return pork to skillet; spoon sauce over pork. Simmer about 2 minutes or until pork is no longer pink in center.

Nutrition Info:

- 260 cal., 8g fat (2.5g sat. fat), 65 chol., 340mg sod., 26g carb. (21g sugars, 1g fiber), 22g pro.

Mediterranean Pasta Caesar Toss

Servings: 4
Cooking Time: 30 Minutes
Ingredients:

- 1 package (9 ounces) refrigerated cheese ravioli
- 1 cup frozen cut green beans, thawed
- 1 cup cherry tomatoes, halved
- 3/4 teaspoon coarsely ground pepper
- 1/3 cup reduced-fat creamy Caesar salad dressing
- 3 tablespoons shredded Parmesan cheese

Directions:

1. In a large saucepan, cook ravioli according to package directions, adding beans during the last 3 minutes of cooking. Drain.
2. In a serving bowl, combine the ravioli mixture, tomatoes and pepper. Add dressing; toss to coat. Sprinkle with cheese.

Nutrition Info:

- 264 cal., 10 g fat (4 g sat. fat), 28 mg chol., 649 mg sodium, 31 g carb., 3 g fiber, 12 g pro.

Simple Teriyaki Steak Dinner

Servings: 4
Cooking Time: 20 Minutes
Ingredients:
- 1 tablespoon butter or margarine
- 1 medium bell pepper (any color), coarsely chopped (1 cup)
- 1½ cups sliced fresh mushrooms (about 5 oz)
- 4 boneless beef top loin steaks (New York, Kansas City or strip steaks), about ¾ inch thick (6 oz each)
- ½ teaspoon garlic salt
- ¼ teaspoon coarse ground black pepper
- ¼ cup teriyaki baste and glaze (from 12-oz bottle)
- 2 tablespoons water

Directions:
1. In 12-inch nonstick skillet, melt butter over medium-high heat. Add bell pepper; cook 2 minutes, stirring frequently. Stir in mushrooms. Cook 2 to 3 minutes, stirring frequently, until vegetables are tender. Remove vegetable mixture from skillet; cover to keep warm.
2. Sprinkle beef steaks with garlic salt and pepper. In same skillet, cook steaks over medium heat 6 to 8 minutes, turning once or twice, until desired doneness.
3. Return vegetables to skillet. Stir teriyaki glaze and water into vegetables and spoon over steaks. Cook about 1 minute, stirring vegetables occasionally, until thoroughly heated.

Nutrition Info:
- 330 cal., 15g fat (6g sat. fat), 80 chol., 600mg sod., 8g carb. (6g sugars, 0g fiber), 41g pro.

Chili-stuffed Potatoes

Servings: 4
Cooking Time: 10 Minutes
Ingredients:
- 4 (8-ounce) baking potatoes, preferably Yukon Gold, scrubbed and pierced several times with a fork
- 12 ounces 90% lean ground beef
- 3/4 cup water
- 1 (1.25-ounce) packet chili seasoning mix

Directions:
1. Microwave the potatoes on HIGH 10–11 minutes or until they are tender when pierced with a fork.
2. Meanwhile, place a large nonstick skillet over medium-high heat until hot. Coat the skillet with nonstick cooking spray, add the beef, and cook until the beef is no longer pink, stirring frequently.
3. Add the water and chili seasoning and stir. Cook 1–2 minutes or until thickened.
4. Split the potatoes almost in half and fluff with a fork. Spoon 1/2 cup chili onto each potato and top with sour cream or cheese (if desired).

Nutrition Info:
- 350 cal., 8g fat (2g sag. fat), 50mg chol, 410mg sod., 48g carb (3g sugars, 5g fiber), 21g pro.

Chili Pork Tenderloin

Servings: 3
Cooking Time: 35 Minutes
Ingredients:
- 1 tablespoon lime juice
- 1 teaspoon chili powder
- 1 teaspoon reduced-sodium soy sauce
- 1/2 teaspoon sugar
- 1/2 teaspoon salt
- 1/4 teaspoon pepper
- 1 pork tenderloin (1 pound)
- 1 tablespoon canola oil

Directions:
1. In a small bowl, combine the first six ingredients; brush over pork. In a large ovenproof skillet, brown pork in oil on all sides.
2. Bake at 375° for 25-30 minutes or until a thermometer reads 145°. Let stand for 5 minutes before slicing.

Nutrition Info:
- 224 cal., 10 g fat (2 g sat. fat), 84 mg chol., 529 mg sodium, 2 g carb., trace fiber, 30 g pro.

Grilled Rosemary Lamb Chops

Servings: 2
Cooking Time: 25 Minutes
Ingredients:
- 1 tablespoon country-style Dijon mustard
- 1 tablespoon chopped fresh rosemary
- 2 teaspoons honey
- 1 clove garlic, finely chopped
- ½ teaspoon salt
- ¼ teaspoon coarse ground black pepper
- 6 French-cut baby lamb chops (1 to 1¼ inches thick)

Directions:
1. Heat gas or charcoal grill. In small bowl, mix all ingredients except lamb. Spread mixture on one side of each lamb chop.
2. Place lamb on grill, coated side up, over medium heat. Cover grill; cook 12 to 15 minutes or until thermometer inserted in center reads 145°F.

Nutrition Info:
- 330 cal., 14g fat (5g sat. fat), 140 chol., 880mg sod., 7g carb. (6g sugars, 0g fiber), 43g pro.

Sriracha-roasted Pork With Sweet Potatoes

Servings: 4
Cooking Time:25 Minutes
Ingredients:
- 1 pound pork tenderloin
- 1 pound sweet potatoes, peeled and cut into 1-inch chunks (1/4 tsp salt and pepper)
- 2 tablespoons honey
- 1 tablespoon hot pepper sauce, such as sriracha

Directions:
1. Preheat oven to 425°F.
2. Heat a large skillet coated with cooking spray over medium-high heat. Add the pork and brown on all sides, about 5 minutes total.
3. Place potatoes in a 13 × 9-inch baking pan. Coat potatoes with cooking spray and toss until well coated. Place the pork in the center of the potatoes and sprinkle 1/4 teaspoon salt and 1/4 teaspoon pepper evenly over all.
4. In a small bowl, combine the honey and sriracha sauce; set aside.
5. Bake 10 minutes, stir potatoes, spoon sauce over pork, and continue baking 15 minutes or until internal temperature of the pork reaches 150°F.
6. Place the pork on a cutting board and let stand 3 minutes before slicing. Meanwhile, gently toss the potatoes in the pan with any pan drippings. Cover to keep warm. Serve with pork.

Nutrition Info:
- 280 cal., 5g fat (1g sag. fat), 75mg chol, 310mg sod., 31g carb (6g sugars, 6g fiber), 26g pro.

Roasted Leg Of Lamb

Servings: 12
Cooking Time: 120 Minutes
Ingredients:
- 1/3 cup olive oil
- 1/4 cup minced fresh rosemary
- 1/4 cup finely chopped onion
- 4 garlic cloves, minced
- 1/2 teaspoon salt
- 1/4 teaspoon pepper
- 1 bone-in leg of lamb (5 to 6 pounds), trimmed

Directions:
1. Preheat oven to 325°. Combine the oil, rosemary, onion, garlic, salt and pepper; rub over lamb. Place fat side up on a rack in a shallow roasting pan.
2. Bake, uncovered, 2 to 2 1/2 hours or until meat reaches desired doneness (for medium-rare, a thermometer should read 145°; medium, 160°; well-done, 170°), basting occasionally with pan juices. Let stand 15 minutes before slicing.

Nutrition Info:
- 212 cal., 12 g fat (3 g sat. fat), 85 mg chol., 137 mg sodium, 1 g carb., trace fiber, 24 g pro.

Smoky Sirloin

Servings: 4
Cooking Time:12 Minutes
Ingredients:

- 1 pound boneless sirloin steak, about 3/4-inch thick
- 1 1/2 teaspoons smoked paprika
- 2 tablespoons Worcestershire sauce
- 2 tablespoons balsamic vinegar

Directions:

1. Sprinkle both sides of the beef with paprika, 1/4 teaspoon salt, and 1/4 teaspoon pepper. Press down lightly to adhere. Let stand 15 minutes at room temperature.
2. Heat a large skillet coated with cooking spray over medium-high heat. Cook beef 4 to 5 minutes on each side. Place on cutting board and let stand 5 minutes before slicing.
3. Combine 1/4 cup water, Worcestershire sauce, and vinegar. Pour into the skillet with any pan residue and bring to a boil over medium-high heat. Boil 2 minutes or until reduced to 2 tablespoons liquid. Pour over sliced beef.

Nutrition Info:

- 150 cal., 3g fat (1g sag. fat), 70mg chol, 280mg sod., 3g carb (2g sugars, 0g fiber), 26g pro.

Homestyle Double-onion Roast

Servings: 6
Cooking Time:1 Hour And 10 Minutes
Ingredients:

- 1 pound carrots, scrubbed, quartered lengthwise, and cut into 3-inch pieces
- 2 medium onions (8 ounces total), cut in 1/2-inch wedges and separated
- 1 3/4 pounds lean eye of round roast
- 1/4 cup water
- 2 1/2 tablespoons onion soup mix

Directions:

1. Preheat the oven to 325°F.
2. Coat a 13 × 9-inch nonstick baking pan with nonstick cooking spray, arrange the carrots and onions in the pan, and set aside.
3. Place a medium nonstick skillet over medium-high heat until hot. Coat the skillet with nonstick cooking spray, add the beef, and brown 2 minutes. Turn and brown another 2 minutes.
4. Place the beef in the center of the baking pan on top of the vegetables. Add the water to the skillet and scrap up the pan drippings, then pour them over the beef. Sprinkle evenly with the soup mix.
5. Cover the pan tightly with foil and cook 1 hour and 5 minutes or until a meat thermometer reaches 135°F. Place the beef on a cutting board and let stand 15 minutes before slicing. (The temperature will rise another 10°F while the beef stands.)
6. Keep the vegetables in the pan covered to keep warm. Place the beef slices on a serving platter, arrange the vegetables around the beef, and spoon the pan liquids evenly over the beef.

Nutrition Info:

- 220 cal., 4g fat (1g sag. fat), 60mg chol, 410mg sod., 13g carb (5g sugars, 3g fiber), 32g pro.

Southwestern Pineapple Pork Chops

Servings: 4
Cooking Time: 30 Minutes
Ingredients:
- 4 boneless pork loin chops (5 ounces each)
- 1/2 teaspoon garlic pepper blend
- 1 tablespoon canola oil
- 1 can (8 ounces) unsweetened crushed pineapple, undrained
- 1 cup medium salsa
- Minced fresh cilantro

Directions:
1. Sprinkle pork chops with pepper blend. In a large skillet, brown chops in oil. Remove and keep warm. In the same skillet, combine pineapple and salsa. Bring to a boil. Return chops to the pan. Reduce heat; cover and simmer for 15-20 minutes or until tender. Sprinkle with cilantro.

Nutrition Info:
- 274 cal., 12 g fat (3 g sat. fat), 68 mg chol., 315 mg sodium, 13 g carb., trace fiber, 27 g pro.

Mom's Sloppy Tacos

Servings: 6
Cooking Time: 30 Minutes
Ingredients:
- 1 1/2 pounds extra-lean ground beef (95% lean)
- 1 can (15 ounces) tomato sauce
- 3/4 teaspoon garlic powder
- 1/2 teaspoon salt
- 1/4 teaspoon pepper
- 1/4 teaspoon cayenne pepper
- 12 taco shells, warmed
- Optional toppings: shredded lettuce and cheese, chopped tomatoes, avocado and olives

Directions:
1. In a large skillet, cook beef over medium heat until no longer pink. Stir in the tomato sauce, garlic powder, salt, pepper and cayenne. Bring to a boil. Reduce heat; simmer, uncovered, for 10 minutes.
2. Fill each taco shell with 1/4 cup beef mixture and toppings of your choice.

Nutrition Info:
- 264 cal., 10 g fat (4 g sat. fat), 65 mg chol., 669 mg sodium, 17 g carb., 1 g fiber, 25 g pro.

Extra-easy Meatballs

Servings: 6
Cooking Time:30 Minutes
Ingredients:
- 1 pound 95% lean ground beef
- 1/2 cup quick-cooking oats
- 3 large egg whites
- 1 (25.5-ounce) jar meatless, fat-free, low-sodium spaghetti sauce (divided use)
- 1/4 teaspoon salt

Directions:
1. Mix the ground beef, oats, egg whites, 1/2 cup spaghetti sauce, and salt together in a large bowl. (You can also add 1 tablespoon dried basil, if desired.) Shape the mixture into 24 (1-inch) meatballs.
2. Place a large nonstick skillet over medium-high heat until hot. Coat with nonstick cooking spray, add the meatballs, and cook until browned, stirring frequently. Use two utensils to stir as you would when stir-frying.
3. Add the remaining spaghetti sauce and bring just to a boil. Reduce the heat, cover tightly, and simmer 20 minutes.

Nutrition Info:
- 170 cal., 4g fat (1g sag. fat), 45mg chol, 180mg sod., 13g carb (7g sugars, 1g fiber), 19g pro.

Sweet Jerk Pork

Servings: 4
Cooking Time:20 Minutes
Ingredients:
- 1 pound pork tenderloin
- 2 teaspoons jerk seasoning
- 2 tablespoons packed dark brown sugar
- 2 teaspoons Worcestershire sauce

Directions:
1. Preheat the oven to 425°F.
2. Sprinkle the pork evenly with the jerk seasoning and press down gently so the spices adhere. Let the pork stand 15 minutes.
3. Stir the sugar and Worcestershire sauce together in a small bowl until well blended. Coat an 11 × 7-inch baking pan with nonstick cooking spray and set aside.
4. Place a large nonstick skillet over medium-high heat until hot. Coat the skillet with nonstick cooking spray, add the pork, and brown all sides, about 5 minutes, turning occasionally.
5. Place the pork in the baking pan and spoon all but 1 tablespoon of the Worcestershire mixture evenly over the pork. Bake for 13–15 minutes or until the pork is barely pink in the center and a meat thermometer reaches 170°F.
6. Place the pork on a cutting board, spoon the remaining 1 tablespoon Worcestershire mixture evenly over all, and let stand 10 minutes before slicing.

Nutrition Info:
- 150 cal., 3g fat (1g sag. fat), 60mg chol, 210mg sod., 8g carb (8g sugars, 0g fiber), 22g pro.

Sausage Pilaf Peppers

Servings: 4
Cooking Time:40 Minutes
Ingredients:
- 4 medium green bell peppers
- 6 ounces reduced-fat pork breakfast sausage
- 3/4 cup uncooked instant brown rice
- 2/3 cup salsa, divided use

Directions:
1. Preheat the oven to 350°F.
2. Slice the tops off of each pepper and discard the seeds and membrane, leaving the peppers whole.
3. Coat a large nonstick skillet with nonstick cooking spray and place over medium-high heat until hot. Add the sausage and cook until it's no longer pink, breaking up large pieces while stirring.
4. Remove from the heat and add the rice and all but 1/4 cup salsa. Stir gently to blend.
5. Fill the peppers with equal amounts of the mixture and top each with 1 tablespoon salsa. Place the peppers in the skillet and cover tightly with foil. Bake 35 minutes or until the peppers are tender.

Nutrition Info:
- 260 cal., 8g fat (2g sag. fat), 20mg chol, 450mg sod., 37g carb (5g sugars, 5g fiber), 11g pro.

Beef Strips With Sweet Ginger Sauce

Servings: 4
Cooking Time:4 Minutes
Ingredients:
- 2 tablespoons lite soy sauce
- 1 tablespoon sugar
- 2 teaspoons grated gingerroot
- 1 pound boneless top round or sirloin steak, trimmed of fat and sliced into strips

Directions:
1. Stir the soy sauce, sugar, and gingerroot together in a small bowl and set aside.
2. Place a large nonstick skillet over medium-high heat until hot. Coat the skillet with nonstick cooking spray, add half the beef, and cook 1 minute, stirring constantly.
3. Remove the beef from the skillet and set aside on a separate plate. Recoat the skillet with nonstick cooking spray and cook the remaining beef 1 minute.
4. Return the first batch of beef to the skillet, add the soy sauce mixture, and cook 1 minute to heat thoroughly.

Nutrition Info:
- 150 cal., 3g fat (1g sag. fat), 60mg chol, 300mg sod., 4g carb (3g sugars, 0g fiber), 24g pro.

Berry Barbecued Pork Roast

Servings: 12
Cooking Time: 75 Minutes
Ingredients:

- 1 boneless rolled pork loin roast (3 pounds)
- 1/4 teaspoon salt
- 1/4 teaspoon pepper
- 4 cups fresh or frozen cranberries
- 1 cup sugar
- 1/2 cup orange juice
- 1/2 cup barbecue sauce

Directions:

1. Sprinkle roast with salt and pepper. Place with fat side up on a rack in a shallow roasting pan. Bake, uncovered, at 350° for 45 minutes.
2. Meanwhile, in a saucepan, combine the cranberries, sugar, orange juice and barbecue sauce. Bring to a boil. Reduce heat to medium-low; cook and stir for 10-12 minutes or until cranberries pop and sauce is thickened.
3. Brush some of the sauce over roast. Bake 15-20 minutes longer or until a thermometer reads 145°, brushing often with sauce. Let meat stand for 10 minutes before slicing. Serve with remaining sauce.

Nutrition Info:

- 262 cal., 8 g fat (3 g sat. fat), 67 mg chol., 190 mg sodium, 23 g carb., 1 g fiber, 24 g pro.

Pork With Caramelized Onions

Servings: 4
Cooking Time: 25 Minutes
Ingredients:

- 1 lb pork tenderloin
- ½ teaspoon salt
- ¼ teaspoon paprika
- 1 large onion, thinly sliced (2 cups)
- ¼ teaspoon sugar

Directions:

1. Cut pork into ½-inch slices. Sprinkle both sides of pork with salt and paprika.
2. Heat 10-inch nonstick skillet over medium-high heat. Add pork; cook 6 to 8 minutes, turning once, until no longer pink in center. Remove pork from skillet; keep warm. Wipe out skillet.
3. Heat same skillet over medium-high heat. Add onion; cook 1 minute, stirring frequently. Reduce heat to medium. Stir in sugar. Cook about 3 minutes longer, stirring frequently, until onion is soft and golden brown. Spoon over pork.

Nutrition Info:

- 170 cal., 4.5g fat (1.5g sat. fat), 70 chol., 350mg sod., 6g carb. (3g sugars, 1g fiber), 26g pro.

Southwest Steak

Servings: 8
Cooking Time: 25 Minutes
Ingredients:

- 1/4 cup lime juice
- 6 garlic cloves, minced
- 4 teaspoons chili powder
- 4 teaspoons canola oil
- 1 teaspoon salt
- 1 teaspoon crushed red pepper flakes
- 1 teaspoon pepper
- 2 beef flank steaks (1 pound each)

Directions:
1. In a large resealable plastic bag, combine the first seven ingredients; add beef. Seal bag and turn to coat; refrigerate for 4 hours or overnight.
2. Drain and discard marinade. Using long-handled tongs, moisten a paper towel with cooking oil and lightly coat the grill rack. Grill the beef, covered, over medium heat or broil 4 in. from the heat for 5-7 minutes on each side or until meat reaches desired doneness (for medium-rare, a thermometer should read 145°; medium, 160°; well-done, 170°).
3. Let stand for 5 minutes; thinly slice across the grain.

Nutrition Info:
- 187 cal., 10 g fat (4 g sat. fat), 54 mg chol., 259 mg sodium, 2 g carb., trace fiber, 22 g pro.

Pan-seared Sirloin Steak

Servings:4
Cooking Time:30 Seconds
Ingredients:

- 1 (1-pound) boneless beef top sirloin steak, 1 to 1½ inches thick, trimmed of all visible fat
- ¼ teaspoon salt
- ⅛ teaspoon pepper
- 2 teaspoons canola oil
- Lemon wedges

Directions:
1. Pat steak dry with paper towels and sprinkle with salt and pepper. Heat oil in 12-inch skillet over medium-high heat until just smoking. Brown steak well on first side, 3 to 5 minutes.
2. Flip steak and continue to cook until meat registers 120 to 125 degrees (for medium-rare), 5 to 10 minutes, reducing heat as needed to prevent scorching. Transfer steak to carving board, tent with aluminum foil, and let rest for 5 minutes. Slice steak thin and serve with lemon wedges.

Nutrition Info:
- 170 cal., 7g fat (2g sag. fat), 70mg chol, 210mg sod., 0g carb (0g sugars, 0g fiber), 25g pro.

Italian Pork And Potato Casserole

Servings: 6
Cooking Time: 45 Minutes
Ingredients:

- 6 cups sliced red potatoes
- 3 tablespoons water
- 1 garlic clove, minced
- 1/2 teaspoon salt
- 1/8 teaspoon pepper
- 6 boneless pork loin chops (6 ounces each)
- 1 jar (24 ounces) marinara sauce
- 1/4 cup shredded Parmesan cheese

Directions:
1. Place potatoes and water in a microwave-safe dish. Cover and microwave on high for 5 minutes or until almost tender; drain.
2. Place potatoes in a 13x9-in. baking dish coated with cooking spray. Sprinkle with garlic, salt and pepper. Top with pork chops and marinara sauce. Cover and bake at 350° for 40-45 minutes or until a thermometer inserted in the pork reads 145° and the potatoes are tender.
3. Sprinkle with cheese. Bake, uncovered, 3-5 minutes longer or until cheese is melted. Let stand 5 minutes before serving.

Nutrition Info:
- 412 cal., 11 g fat (4 g sat. fat), 84 mg chol., 506 mg sodium, 38 g carb., 4 g fiber, 39 g pro.

Easy & Elegant Tenderloin Roast

Servings:12
Cooking Time: 50 Minutes
Ingredients:

- 1 beef tenderloin (5 pounds)
- 2 tablespoons olive oil
- 4 garlic cloves, minced
- 2 teaspoons sea salt
- 1 1/2 teaspoons coarsely ground pepper

Directions:
1. Preheat oven to 425°. Place roast on a rack in a shallow roasting pan. In a small bowl, mix the oil, garlic, salt and pepper; rub over roast.
2. Roast 50-70 minutes or until meat reaches desired doneness (for medium-rare, a thermometer should read 145°; medium, 160°). Remove from oven; tent with foil. Let stand 15 minutes before slicing.

Nutrition Info:
- 294 cal., 13g fat (5g sat. fat), 82mg chol., 394mg sod., 1g carb. (0 sugars, 0 fiber), 40g pro.

Grilled Dijon Pork Roast

Servings:12
Cooking Time: 1 Hour
Ingredients:

- 1/3 cup balsamic vinegar
- 3 tablespoons Dijon mustard
- 1 tablespoon honey
- 1 teaspoon salt
- 1 boneless pork loin roast (3 to 4 pounds)

Directions:

1. In a large resealable plastic bag, whisk vinegar, mustard, honey and salt. Add pork; seal the bag and turn to coat. Refrigerate for at least 8 hours or overnight.
2. Prepare grill for indirect heat, using a drip pan.
3. Drain pork, discarding marinade. Place pork on a greased grill rack over drip pan and cook, covered, over indirect medium heat for 1 to 1 1/2 hours or until a thermometer reads 145°, turning occasionally. Let stand for 10 minutes before slicing.

Nutrition Info:

- 149 cal., 5g fat (2g sat. fat), 56mg chol., 213mg sod., 2g carb. (1g sugars, 0 fiber), 22g pro.

Pork With Tomato Caper Sauce

Servings: 4
Cooking Time:10 Minutes
Ingredients:

- 2 tablespoons tomato paste with oregano, basil, and garlic
- 2 tablespoons capers, drained and mashed with a fork
- 2/3 cup water, divided use
- 1/8 teaspoon salt
- 4 (4-ounce) boneless pork chops, trimmed of fat

Directions:

1. Using a fork, stir the tomato paste, capers, and 1/3 cup water together in a small bowl.
2. Place a medium nonstick skillet over medium-high heat until hot. Coat the skillet with nonstick cooking spray, add the pork chops, and cook 3 minutes.
3. Turn the pork chops and immediately reduce the heat to medium. Spoon the tomato mixture evenly on top of each pork chop, cover tightly, and cook 5 minutes or until the pork chops are barely pink in the center. The sauce may be dark in some areas.
4. Remove the skillet from the heat and add the remaining 1/3 cup water and salt. Turn the pork chops over several times to remove the sauce. Place the pork chops on a serving plate and set aside.
5. Increase the heat to medium high. Bring the sauce to a boil, stirring constantly, and boil 1 minute or until the sauce begins to thicken slightly and measures 1/2 cup. Spoon the sauce over the pork chops.

Nutrition Info:

- 140 cal., 3g fat (1g sag. fat), 65mg chol, 330mg sod., 2g carb (1g sugars, 0g fiber), 25g pro.

Sweet Sherry'd Pork Tenderloin

Servings: 4
Cooking Time:22 Minutes
Ingredients:

- 1 pound pork tenderloin
- 1/4 cup dry sherry (divided use)
- 3 tablespoons lite soy sauce (divided use)
- 1/3 cup peach all-fruit spread

Directions:

1. Place the pork, 2 tablespoons sherry, and 2 tablespoons soy sauce in a quart-sized zippered plastic bag. Seal tightly and toss back and forth to coat evenly. Refrigerate overnight or at least 8 hours.
2. Stir the fruit spread, 2 tablespoons sherry, and 1 tablespoon soy sauce together in a small bowl. Cover with plastic wrap and refrigerate until needed.
3. Preheat the oven to 425°F.
4. Remove the pork from the marinade and discard the marinade. Place a medium nonstick skillet over medium-high heat until hot. Coat the skillet with nonstick cooking spray, add the pork, and brown on all sides.
5. Place the pork in a 9-inch pie pan and bake 15 minutes or until the pork is barely pink in the center. Place the pork on a cutting board and let stand 3 minutes before slicing.
6. Meanwhile, place the fruit spread mixture in the skillet and bring to a boil over medium-high heat, stirring frequently. Place the sauce on the bottom of a serving plate and arrange the pork on top. Sprinkle evenly with black pepper, if desired.

Nutrition Info:

- 190 cal., 3g fat (1g sag. fat), 60mg chol, 320mg sod., 14g carb (11g sugars, 0g fiber), 23g pro.

Sizzling Pork Chops

Servings: 4
Cooking Time:12 Minutes
Ingredients:

- 4 (4-ounce) boneless pork chops, trimmed of fat
- 1 tablespoon dried zesty Italian salad dressing and recipe mix (available in packets)

Directions:

1. Coat both sides of the pork chops with the salad dressing mix, pressing down gently so the spices adhere.
2. Place a large nonstick skillet over medium heat until hot. Coat the skillet with nonstick cooking spray, add the pork, and cook 4 minutes. Turn and cook 4 minutes longer or until the pork is barely pink in the center.
3. Remove the skillet from the heat and let the pork stand in the skillet 2–3 minutes or until the pork begins to release some of its juices. Move the pork pieces around in the skillet several times to absorb the pan residue.

Nutrition Info:

- 140 cal., 3g fat (1g sag. fat), 65mg chol, 390mg sod., 1g carb (1g sugars, 0g fiber), 25g pro.

Chapter 5. Poultry Recipes

Lemon Chicken With Olives

Servings: 4
Cooking Time: 20 Minutes
Ingredients:

- 4 boneless skinless chicken breast halves (about 1¼ lb)
- 2 teaspoons olive or canola oil
- 1 tablespoon lemon juice
- 1 teaspoon salt-free lemon-pepper seasoning
- ¼ cup sliced ripe olives
- 4 thin slices lemon

Directions:

1. Set oven control to broil. Spray broiler pan rack with cooking spray. Starting at thickest edge of each chicken breast, cut horizontally almost to opposite side. Open cut chicken breast so it is an even thickness.
2. In small bowl, mix oil and lemon juice. Drizzle over both sides of chicken breasts. Sprinkle both sides with lemon-pepper seasoning. Place on rack in broiler pan.
3. Broil with tops 4 inches from heat about 10 minutes, turning once, until chicken is no longer pink in center. During last 2 minutes of broiling, top with olives and lemon slices.

Nutrition Info:

- 200 cal., 8g fat (1.5g sat. fat), 85 chol., 150mg sod., 1g carb. (0g sugars, 0g fiber), 31g pro.

Honey-mustard Turkey Breast

Servings: 12
Cooking Time: 115 Minutes
Ingredients:

- 1 bone-in turkey breast (5 to 6 pounds)
- 1/2 cup honey mustard
- 3/4 teaspoon dried rosemary, crushed
- 1/2 teaspoon onion powder
- 1/4 teaspoon salt
- 1/8 teaspoon garlic powder
- 1/8 teaspoon pepper

Directions:

1. Place the turkey breast, skin side up, on a rack in a foil-lined shallow roasting pan. In a small bowl, combine the remaining ingredients. Spoon over the turkey.
2. Bake, uncovered, at 325° for 1 3/4 to 2 1/2 hours or until a thermometer reads 170°, basting every 30 minutes. Cover and let stand for 10 minutes before slicing.
3. HONEY-APPLE TURKEY BREAST Omit honey mustard and seasonings. Heat 3/4 cup thawed apple juice concentrate, 1/3 cup honey and 1 tablespoon ground mustard over low heat for 2-3 minutes or just until blended, stirring occasionally. Prepare the turkey as directed in a foil-lined pan. Pour honey mixture over turkey. Proceed as directed, basting with pan juices every 30 minutes. (Cover loosely with foil if turkey browns too quickly.)

Nutrition Info:

- 283 cal., 11 g fat (3 g sat. fat), 102 mg chol., 221 mg sodium, 5 g carb., trace fiber, 40 g pro.

Cheesy Chicken And Rice

Servings: 4
Cooking Time:12 Minutes
Ingredients:
- 1 1/2 cups water
- 1 cup instant brown rice
- 12 ounces frozen broccoli and cauliflower florets
- 12 ounces boneless, skinless chicken breast, rinsed and patted dry, cut into bite-sized pieces
- 3 ounces reduced-fat processed cheese (such as Velveeta), cut in 1/2-inch cubes

Directions:
1. Bring the water to boil in a large saucepan, then add the rice and vegetables. Return to a boil, reduce the heat, cover tightly, and simmer 10 minutes or until the liquid is absorbed.
2. Meanwhile, place a large nonstick skillet over medium heat until hot. Coat the skillet with nonstick cooking spray and add the chicken. Cook 10 minutes or until the chicken is no longer pink in the center and is just beginning to lightly brown on the edges, stirring frequently.
3. Add the chicken, cheese, 1/8 teaspoon salt, if desired, and pepper to the rice mixture and stir until the cheese has melted. Add pepper to taste, if desired.

Nutrition Info:
- 340 cal., 6g fat (1g sag. fat), 55mg chol, 380mg sod., 43g carb (4g sugars, 4g fiber), 28g pro.

Peach Barbecued Chicken

Servings: 4
Cooking Time:18 Minutes
Ingredients:
- 8 chicken drumsticks, skin removed, rinsed and patted dry (about 2 pounds total)
- 2 tablespoons peach all-fruit spread
- 1/4 cup barbeque sauce, preferably hickory- or mesquite-flavored
- 2 teaspoons grated gingerroot

Directions:
1. Preheat the broiler.
2. Coat a broiler rack and pan with nonstick cooking spray. Arrange the drumsticks on the rack and broil about 4 inches away from heat source for 8 minutes. Turn and broil 6 minutes or until the juices run clear.
3. Meanwhile, place the fruit spread in a small glass bowl and microwave on HIGH 20 seconds or until the fruit spread has melted slightly. Add the barbeque sauce and ginger and stir to blend. Place 1 tablespoon of the mixture in a separate small bowl and set aside.
4. When the chicken is cooked, brush with half of the sauce and broil 2 minutes. Turn the drumsticks, brush with the remaining half of the sauce, and broil 2 more minutes.
5. Remove the drumsticks from the broiler, turn them over, and brush with the reserved 1 tablespoon sauce to serve.

Nutrition Info:
- 230 cal., 6g fat (1g sag. fat), 95mg chol, 220mg sod., 13g carb (10g sugars, 0g fiber), 29g pro.

Dijon'd Chicken With Rosemary

Servings: 4
Cooking Time:13 Minutes
Ingredients:
- 1 tablespoon Dijon mustard
- 1 tablespoon extra virgin olive oil
- 1/4 teaspoon dried rosemary
- 4 (4-ounce) boneless, skinless chicken breasts, rinsed and patted dry

Directions:
1. Using a fork, stir the mustard, olive oil, and rosemary together in a small bowl until well blended and set aside.
2. Place a medium nonstick skillet over medium heat until hot. Coat the skillet with nonstick cooking spray, add the chicken, and cook 5 minutes.
3. Turn the chicken, then spoon equal amounts of the mustard mixture over each piece. Reduce the heat to medium low, cover tightly, and cook 7 minutes or until the chicken is no longer pink in the center.
4. Turn the chicken several times to blend the mustard mixture with the pan drippings, place the chicken on a serving platter, and spoon the mustard mixture over all.

Nutrition Info:
- 160 cal., 6g fat (1g sag. fat), 65mg chol, 150mg sod., 1g carb (0g sugars, 0g fiber), 24g pro.

In-a-pinch Chicken & Spinach

Servings:4
Cooking Time: 25 Minutes
Ingredients:
- 4 boneless skinless chicken breast halves (6 ounces each)
- 2 tablespoons olive oil
- 1 tablespoon butter
- 1 package (6 ounces) fresh baby spinach
- 1 cup salsa

Directions:
1. Pound chicken with a meat mallet to 1/2-in. thickness. In a large skillet, heat oil and butter over medium heat. Cook the chicken for 5-6 minutes on each side or until no longer pink. Remove chicken and keep warm.
2. Add spinach and salsa to pan; cook and stir 3-4 minutes or just until spinach is wilted. Serve with chicken.

Nutrition Info:
- 297 cal., 14g fat (4g sat. fat), 102mg chol., 376mg sod., 6g carb. (2g sugars, 1g fiber), 36g pro.

Slow Cooker Turkey Breast

Servings: 14
Cooking Time: 300 Minutes
Ingredients:
- 1 bone-in turkey breast (6 to 7 pounds), skin removed
- 1 tablespoon olive oil
- 1 teaspoon dried minced garlic
- 1 teaspoon seasoned salt
- 1 teaspoon paprika
- 1 teaspoon Italian seasoning
- 1 teaspoon pepper
- 1/2 cup water

Directions:
1. Brush turkey with oil. Combine the garlic, seasoned salt, paprika, Italian seasoning and pepper; rub over turkey. Transfer to a 6-qt. slow cooker; add water. Cover and cook on low for 5-6 hours or until tender.

Nutrition Info:
- 174 cal., 2 g fat (trace sat. fat), 101 mg chol., 172 mg sodium, trace carb., trace fiber, 37 g pro.

Cranberry-glazed Turkey Breast

Servings: 12
Cooking Time: 110 Minutes
Ingredients:
- 1 1/4 cups jellied cranberry sauce
- 2/3 cup thawed unsweetened apple juice concentrate
- 2 tablespoons butter
- 1 bone-in turkey breast (5 to 6 pounds)

Directions:
1. In a small saucepan, bring the cranberry sauce, apple juice concentrate and butter to a boil. Remove from the heat; cool.
2. Carefully loosen skin of turkey breast. Set aside 1/2 cup sauce for basting and 3/4 cup for serving. Spoon remaining sauce onto the turkey, rubbing mixture under and over skin.
3. Place turkey on a rack in a shallow roasting pan. Bake, uncovered, at 325° for 1 1/2 to 2 hours or until a thermometer reads 170°, basting occasionally with reserved sauce. Cover and let stand for 10 minutes before carving. Warm reserved 3/4 cup of sauce; serve with turkey.

Nutrition Info:
- 244 cal., 3 g fat (1 g sat. fat), 103 mg chol., 91 mg sodium, 17 g carb., trace fiber, 36 g pro.

Weeknight Skillet Roast Chicken

Servings:4
Cooking Time:x
Ingredients:

- 1 (4-pound) whole chicken, giblets discarded
- 1 tablespoon canola oil
- ½ teaspoon kosher salt
- ½ teaspoon pepper
- Lemon wedges

Directions:

1. Adjust oven rack to middle position, place 12-inch oven-safe skillet on rack, and heat oven to 450 degrees. Pat chicken dry with paper towels. Rub entire surface with oil and sprinkle with salt and pepper. Tie legs together with twine and tuck wing tips behind back.
2. Transfer chicken breast side up to hot skillet in oven. Roast chicken until breast registers 120 degrees and thighs register 135 degrees, 25 to 35 minutes. Turn oven off and leave chicken in oven until breast registers 160 degrees and thighs register 175 degrees, 25 to 35 minutes.
3. Transfer chicken to carving board and let rest for 20 minutes. Carve chicken, discard skin, and serve with lemon wedges.

Nutrition Info:

- 240 cal., 6g fat (1g sag. fat), 160mg chol, 280mg sod., 0g carb (0g sugars, 0g fiber), 42g pro.

Greek Chicken With Lemon

Servings: 4
Cooking Time:50 Minutes
Ingredients:

- 8 chicken drumsticks, skin removed, rinsed and patted dry
- 2 tablespoons dried salt-free Greek seasoning (sold in jars in the spice aisle)
- 2 teaspoons extra virgin olive oil
- 1 teaspoon lemon zest
- 4 tablespoons lemon juice (divided use)

Directions:

1. Place the drumsticks, Greek seasoning, olive oil, lemon zest, and 2 tablespoons lemon juice in a gallon-sized zippered plastic bag. Seal the bag and toss back and forth to coat the chicken evenly. Refrigerate for 8 hours or up to 48 hours, turning occasionally.
2. Preheat the oven to 350°F.
3. Coat a 12 × 8-inch baking dish with nonstick cooking spray, arrange the drumsticks in a single layer, and pour the marinade evenly over all. Bake uncovered for 50–55 minutes or until the drumsticks are no longer pink in the center, turning occasionally.
4. Place the drumsticks on a serving platter. Add salt to taste, if desired, and 2 tablespoons lemon juice to a small bowl, stir to blend well, and pour evenly over the chicken pieces. Season with 1/8 teaspoon salt, if desired.

Nutrition Info:

- 210 cal., 8g fat (1g sag. fat), 95mg chol, 100mg sod., 2g carb (0g sugars, 1g fiber), 30g pro.

Grilled Lemon-rosemary Chicken

Servings: 6
Cooking Time: 25 Minutes
Ingredients:
- 1/4 cup lemon juice
- 3 tablespoons honey
- 2 teaspoons canola oil
- 1 teaspoon dried rosemary, crushed
- 1/2 teaspoon salt
- 1/8 teaspoon pepper
- 6 boneless skinless chicken breast halves (6 ounces each)

Directions:

1. In a large resealable plastic bag, combine the first six ingredients. Add the chicken; seal bag and turn to coat. Refrigerate for 2 hours.
2. Drain and discard marinade. Moisten a paper towel with cooking oil; using long-handled tongs, lightly coat the grill rack. Grill chicken, covered, over medium heat or broil 4 in. from the heat for 6-8 minutes on each side or until a thermometer reads 170°.

Nutrition Info:
- 187 cal., 4 g fat (1 g sat. fat), 94 mg chol., 102 mg sodium, 1 g carb., trace fiber, 34 g pro.

Turkey & Apricot Wraps

Servings:4
Cooking Time: 15 Minutes
Ingredients:
- 1/2 cup reduced-fat cream cheese
- 3 tablespoons apricot preserves
- 4 whole wheat tortillas (8 inches), room temperature
- 1/2 pound sliced reduced-sodium deli turkey
- 2 cups fresh baby spinach or arugula

Directions:

1. In a small bowl, mix cream cheese and preserves. Spread about 2 tablespoons over each tortilla to within 1/2 in. of edges. Layer with turkey and spinach. Roll up tightly. Serve immediately or wrap in plastic wrap and refrigerate until serving.

Nutrition Info:
- 312 cal., 10g fat (4g sat. fat), 41mg chol., 655mg sod., 33g carb. (8g sugars, 2g fiber), 20g pro.

Honey-of-a-meal Chicken

Servings: 4
Cooking Time: 30 Minutes
Ingredients:
- 4 bone-in chicken breast halves, skin removed (8 ounces each)
- 2 tablespoons olive oil
- 1 medium onion, finely chopped
- 1 cup chicken broth
- 2 tablespoons spicy brown mustard
- 1/2 teaspoon pepper
- 2 tablespoons honey

Directions:
1. In a pressure cooker, brown chicken breasts in oil in batches. Set chicken aside. Saute onion in the drippings until tender. Stir in the broth, mustard and pepper. Return chicken to the pan. Close cover securely according to manufacturer's directions.
2. Bring cooker to full pressure over high heat. Reduce heat to medium-high and cook for 8 minutes. (Pressure regulator should maintain a slow steady rocking motion or release of steam; adjust heat if needed.) Immediately cool according to manufacturer's directions until the pressure is completely reduced. Remove chicken and keep warm.
3. Stir honey into sauce. Bring to a boil. Reduce heat; simmer, uncovered, for 8-10 minutes or until thickened. Serve with the chicken.

Nutrition Info:
- 314 cal., 11 g fat (2 g sat. fat), 103 mg chol., 433 mg sodium, 13 g carb., 1 g fiber, 38 g pro.

Chicken Sausages With Peppers

Servings: 4
Cooking Time: 30 Minutes
Ingredients:
- 1 small onion, halved and sliced
- 1 small sweet orange pepper, julienned
- 1 small sweet red pepper, julienned
- 1 tablespoon olive oil
- 1 garlic clove, minced
- 1 package (12 ounces) fully cooked apple chicken sausage links or flavor of your choice, cut into 1-inch pieces

Directions:
1. In a large nonstick skillet, saute onion and peppers in oil until crisp-tender. Add garlic; cook 1 minute longer. Stir in sausages; heat through.

Nutrition Info:
- 208 cal., 11 g fat (2 g sat. fat), 60 mg chol., 483 mg sodium, 14 g carb., 1 g fiber, 15 g pro.

Turkey With Cranberry Sauce

Servings: 15
Cooking Time: 240 Minutes
Ingredients:

- 2 boneless skinless turkey breast halves (3 pounds each)
- 1 can (14 ounces) jellied cranberry sauce
- 1/2 cup plus 2 tablespoons water, divided
- 1 envelope onion soup mix
- 2 tablespoons cornstarch

Directions:
1. Place turkey breasts in a 5-qt. slow cooker. In a large bowl, combine the cranberry sauce, 1/2 cup water and soup mix. Pour over turkey. Cover and cook on low for 4-6 hours or meat is tender. Remove turkey and keep warm.
2. Transfer cooking juices to a large saucepan. Combine the cornstarch and remaining water until smooth. Bring cranberry mixture to a boil; gradually stir in cornstarch mixture until smooth. Cook and stir for 2 minutes or until thickened. Slice turkey; serve with cranberry sauce.

Nutrition Info:
- 248 cal., 1 g fat (trace sat. fat), 112 mg chol., 259 mg sodium, 12 g carb., trace fiber, 45 g pro.

Rustic Mexican Chicken And Rice

Servings: 4
Cooking Time:8 Hours
Ingredients:

- 1 pound boneless, skinless chicken thighs, trimmed of fat
- 1 (10-ounce) can diced tomatoes with green chilies
- 3/4 cup instant brown rice
- 2 tablespoons extra-virgin olive oil

Directions:
1. Combine chicken and tomatoes in a 3 1/2 to 4-quart slow cooker, cover, and cook on low setting for 7–8 hours or on high setting for 3 1/2–4 hours.
2. Gently stir in rice and 3/4 cup hot water, cover, and cook on high for 20 minutes.
3. Drizzle oil evenly over all and sprinkle with 1/8 teaspoon salt.

Nutrition Info:
- 250 cal., 12g fat (2g sag. fat), 110mg chol, 510mg sod., 12g carb (0g sugars, 1g fiber), 24g pro.

Turkey Patties With Dark Onion Gravy

Servings: 4
Cooking Time:20 Minutes
Ingredients:

- 1 pound 93% lean ground turkey
- 1 tablespoon flour
- 1 1/3 cups chopped yellow onion
- 1 tablespoon sodium-free chicken bouillon granules

Directions:

1. Shape the turkey into 4 patties, about 1/2 inch thick; sprinkle with 1/8 teaspoon salt and 1/8 teaspoon pepper, if desired.
2. Heat a large skillet over medium-high heat. Add flour and cook 3 minutes or until beginning to lightly brown, stirring constantly. Set aside on separate plate.
3. Coat skillet with cooking spray, add onions, and cook 3 minutes or until beginning to brown on edges. Push to one side of the skillet, add the turkey patties, reduce to medium heat, and cook 6 minutes on each side or until no longer pink in center.
4. Remove the turkey patties from the onion mixture and set aside on serving platter. Add 1 cup water and bouillon granules to the onions, sprinkle with the flour and 1/8 teaspoon salt and 1/8 teaspoon pepper. Stir and cook until thickened, about 1 1/2 to 2 minutes. Spoon over patties.

Nutrition Info:

- 210 cal., 10g fat (2g sag. fat), 84mg chol, 230mg sod., 8g carb (2g sugars, 1g fiber), 22g pro.

Taco Chicken Tenders

Servings: 4
Cooking Time:7 Minutes
Ingredients:

- 4 teaspoons taco seasoning mix (available in packets)
- 1 pound chicken tenderloins, rinsed and patted dry
- 1/2 medium lime
- 2 tablespoons fat-free sour cream

Directions:

1. Sprinkle the taco seasoning evenly over both sides of the chicken pieces, pressing down gently so the spices adhere.
2. Place a large nonstick skillet over medium-high heat until hot. Coat the skillet with nonstick cooking spray, add the chicken, and cook 2 minutes.
3. Turn gently to keep the seasonings on the chicken as much as possible, reduce the heat to medium, and cook 2 minutes. Turn gently and cook 2 more minutes or until the chicken is no longer pink in the center.
4. Remove from the heat, squeeze lime juice evenly over all, and serve with 1/2 tablespoon sour cream per serving.

Nutrition Info:

- 140 cal., 3g fat (0g sag. fat), 65mg chol, 290mg sod., 3g carb (1g sugars, 1g fiber), 24g pro.

Molasses Drumsticks With Soy Sauce

Servings: 4
Cooking Time:25 Minutes
Ingredients:

- 2 1/2 tablespoons lite soy sauce
- 1 1/4 tablespoons lime juice
- 8 chicken drumsticks, skin removed, rinsed, and patted dry
- 2 tablespoons dark molasses

Directions:
1. Stir the soy sauce and lime juice together in a small bowl until well blended.
2. Place the drumsticks in a large zippered plastic bag. Add 2 tablespoons of the soy sauce mixture to the bag. Seal tightly and shake back and forth to coat chicken evenly. Refrigerate overnight or at least 2 hours, turning occasionally.
3. Add the molasses to the remaining soy sauce mixture, cover with plastic wrap, and refrigerate until needed.
4. Preheat the broiler. Lightly coat the broiler rack and pan with nonstick cooking spray, place the drumsticks on the rack, and discard any marinade in the bag. Broil 6 inches away from the heat source for 25 minutes, turning every 5 minutes or until the drumsticks are no longer pink in the center.
5. Place the drumsticks in a large bowl. Stir the reserved soy sauce mixture and pour it over the drumsticks. Toss the drumsticks gently to coat evenly and let them stand 3 minutes to develop flavors.

Nutrition Info:
- 210 cal., 6g fat (1g sag. fat), 95mg chol, 450mg sod., 6g carb (4g sugars, 0g fiber), 30g pro.

Smoked Turkey Breast

Servings:12
Cooking Time:x
Ingredients:

- 1 (5-pound) bone-in turkey breast
- ¼ cup salt
- 1 teaspoon pepper
- 2 cups wood chips
- 1 (13 by 9-inch) disposable aluminum roasting pan (if using charcoal)

Directions:
1. To remove backbone, use kitchen shears to cut through ribs following vertical line of fat where breast meets back, from tapered end of breast to wing joint. Using your hands, bend back away from breast to pop shoulder joint out of socket. With paring knife, cut through joint between bones to separate back from breast; discard backbone. Trim excess fat from breast. Dissolve salt in 4 quarts cold water in large container. Submerge turkey breast in brine, cover, and refrigerate for at least 3 hours or up to 6 hours.
2. Just before grilling, soak wood chips in water for 15 minutes, then drain. Using large piece of heavy-duty aluminum foil, wrap soaked chips in foil packet and cut several vent holes in top. Remove turkey from brine, pat dry with paper towels, and sprinkle with pepper. Poke skin all over with skewer.
3. FOR A CHARCOAL GRILL Open bottom vent halfway and place disposable pan in center of grill. Light large chimney starter filled with charcoal briquettes (6 quarts). When top coals are partially covered with ash, pour into 2 even piles on either side of disposable pan. Place wood chip packet on coals. Set cooking grate in place, cover, and open lid vent halfway. Heat grill until hot and wood chips are smoking, about 5 minutes.
4. FOR A GAS GRILL Remove cooking grate and place wood chip packet directly on primary burner. Set cooking grate in place, turn all burners to high, cover, and heat grill until hot and wood chips are smoking, about 15 minutes. Turn all burners to medium-low. (Adjust burners as needed to maintain grill temperature around 350 degrees.)
5. Clean and oil cooking grate. Place turkey breast, skin side up, in center of grill (over disposable pan if using charcoal). Cover (position lid vent over turkey if using charcoal) and cook until skin is well browned and breast registers 160 degrees, about 1½ hours.
6. Transfer turkey to carving board and let rest for 20 minutes. Carve turkey, discard skin, and serve.

Nutrition Info:
- 170 cal., 2g fat (0g sag. fat), 85mg chol, 310mg sod., 0g carb (0g sugars, 0g fiber), 35g pro.

Easy Roast Turkey Breast

Servings:12
Cooking Time:30 Minutes
Ingredients:

* 1 (5-pound) bone-in turkey breast
* ¼ cup salt
* 1 teaspoon pepper

Directions:

1. To remove backbone, use kitchen shears to cut through ribs following vertical line of fat where breast meets back, from tapered end of breast to wing joint. Using your hands, bend back away from breast to pop shoulder joint out of socket. With paring knife, cut through joint between bones to separate back from breast; discard backbone. Trim excess fat from breast. Dissolve salt in 4 quarts cold water in large container. Submerge turkey breast in brine, cover, and refrigerate for at least 3 hours or up to 6 hours.
2. Adjust oven rack to middle position and heat oven to 425 degrees. Set V-rack inside roasting pan and spray with vegetable oil spray. Remove turkey from brine, pat dry with paper towels, and sprinkle with pepper. Place turkey, skin side up, on prepared V-rack and add 1 cup water to pan. Roast turkey for 30 minutes.
3. Reduce oven temperature to 325 degrees and continue to roast until turkey registers 160 degrees, about 1 hour. Transfer turkey to carving board and let rest for 20 minutes. Carve turkey, discard skin, and serve.

Nutrition Info:

* 170 cal., 2g fat (0g sag. fat), 85mg chol, 310mg sod., 0g carb (0g sugars, 0g fiber), 35g pro.

Chicken Apple Sausage And Onion Smothered Grits

Servings: 4
Cooking Time:10 Minutes
Ingredients:

* 2/3 cup dry quick cooking grits
* 8 ounces sliced fresh mushrooms
* 3 (4 ounces each) links fully cooked chicken apple sausage, thinly sliced, such as Al Fresco
* 1 1/2 cups chopped onion

Directions:

1. Bring 2 2/3 cups water to a boil in a medium saucepan. Slowly stir in the grits, reduce heat to medium-low, cover, and cook 5–7 minutes or until thickened.
2. Meanwhile, heat a large skillet coated with cooking spray over medium-high heat. Add the mushrooms and cook 4 minutes or until beginning to lightly brown. Set aside on separate plate.
3. Coat skillet with cooking spray and cook sausage 3 minutes or until browned on edges, stirring occasionally. Set aside with mushrooms. To pan residue, add onions, coat with cooking spray, and cook 4 minutes or until richly browned. Add the sausage and mushrooms back to the skillet with any accumulated juices and 1/4 cup water. Cook 1 minute to heat through.
4. Sprinkle with 1/8 teaspoon salt and 1/8 teaspoon pepper. Spoon equal amounts of the grits in each of 4 shallow soup bowls, top with the sausage mixture.

Nutrition Info:

* 270 cal., 7g fat (1g sag. fat), 60mg chol, 430mg sod., 31g carb (4g sugars, 3g fiber), 19g pro.

Panko Ranch Chicken Strips With Dipping Sauce

Servings: 4
Cooking Time:12 Minutes
Ingredients:
- 8 chicken tenderloins, about 1 pound total
- 3/4 cup yogurt ranch dressing, divided use
- 3/4 cup panko breadcrumbs
- 3 tablespoons canola oil

Directions:
1. Place chicken in a medium bowl with 1/4 cup of the ranch dressing; toss until well coated. Place the breadcrumbs in a shallow pan, such as a pie pan. Coat chicken pieces, one at a time with the breadcrumbs and set aside.
2. Heat oil in a large skillet over medium-high heat. Add the chicken and immediately reduce to medium-low heat, cook 12 minutes or until golden and no longer pink in center, gently turning occasionally.
3. Remove from skillet, sprinkle with 1/8 teaspoon salt. Serve with remaining 1/2 cup ranch for dipping.

Nutrition Info:
- 340 cal., 16g fat (2g sag. fat), 85mg chol, 390mg sod., 17g carb (4g sugars, 1g fiber), 30g pro.

Hoisin Chicken

Servings: 4
Cooking Time:8 Minutes
Ingredients:
- 3 tablespoons hoisin sauce
- 1 teaspoon orange zest
- 3 tablespoons orange juice
- 1 pound boneless, skinless chicken breasts, rinsed, patted dry, and cut into thin slices or strips

Directions:
1. Stir the hoisin sauce, orange zest, and juice together in a small bowl and set aside.
2. Place a medium nonstick skillet over medium-high heat until hot. Coat the skillet with nonstick cooking spray, add the chicken, and cook 6–7 minutes or until the chicken just begins to lightly brown. Use two utensils to stir as you would when stir-frying.
3. Place the chicken on a serving platter. Add the hoisin mixture to the skillet and cook 15 seconds, stirring constantly. Spoon evenly over the chicken.

Nutrition Info:
- 160 cal., 3g fat (0g sag. fat), 65mg chol, 260mg sod., 7g carb (4g sugars, 0g fiber), 24g pro.

Avocado And Green Chili Chicken

Servings: 4
Cooking Time:22 Minutes
Ingredients:

- 4 (4 ounces each) boneless, skinless chicken breast, flattened to 1/2-inch thickness
- 1 (4-ounce) can chopped mild green chilies
- 1 ripe medium avocado, chopped
- 1 lime, halved

Directions:

1. Preheat oven to 400°F.
2. Place chicken in an 11 × 7-inch baking pan, squeeze half of the lime over all. Spoon green chilies on top of each breast and spread over all. Bake, uncovered, 22–25 minutes or until chicken is no longer pink in center.
3. Top with avocado, squeeze remaining lime half over all, and sprinkle evenly with 1/4 teaspoon salt and 1/4 teaspoon pepper.

Nutrition Info:

- 200 cal., 8g fat (1g sag. fat), 85mg chol, 310mg sod., 6g carb (1g sugars, 3g fiber), 27g pro.

Sausage And Farro Mushrooms

Servings: 4
Cooking Time:20 Minutes
Ingredients:

- 1/2 cup dry pearled farro
- 2 (3.9 ounces each) Italian turkey sausage links, removed from casing, such as Jennie-o
- 8 portabella mushroom caps, stems removed, caps wiped with damp cloth
- 2 tablespoons crumbled reduced-fat blue cheese

Directions:

1. Preheat broiler. Coat both sides of the mushrooms with cooking spray, place on a foil-lined baking sheet, and broil 5 minutes on each side or until tender.
2. Meanwhile, heat a large nonstick skillet over medium-high heat, add sausage, and cook 3 minutes or until browned, breaking up larger pieces while cooking. Set aside on separate plate.
3. Add 2 cups water and the farro to any pan residue in skillet, bring to a boil, reduce heat to medium-low, cover, and simmer 15 minutes or until slightly "chewy." Stir in the sausage and cheese; cook, uncovered, for 2 minutes to thicken slightly. Spoon equal amounts into each mushroom cap and sprinkle with black pepper.

Nutrition Info:

- 200 cal., 6g fat (1g sag. fat), 30mg chol, 390mg sod., 23g carb (2g sugars, 3g fiber), 16g pro.

Grilled Basil Chicken And Tomatoes

Servings: 4
Cooking Time: 25 Minutes
Ingredients:
- 8 plum tomatoes, divided
- 3/4 cup balsamic vinegar
- 1/4 cup tightly packed fresh basil leaves
- 2 tablespoons olive oil
- 1 garlic clove, minced
- 1/2 teaspoon salt
- 4 boneless skinless chicken breast halves (4 ounces each)

Directions:
1. Cut four tomatoes into quarters and place in a food processor. Add the vinegar, basil, oil, garlic and salt; cover and process until blended.
2. Pour 1/2 cup dressing into a small bowl; cover and refrigerate until serving. Pour remaining dressing into a large resealable plastic bag; add chicken. Seal bag and turn to coat; refrigerate for up to 1 hour.
3. Drain and discard marinade. Using long-handled tongs, moisten a paper towel with cooking oil and lightly coat the grill rack. Grill chicken, covered, over medium heat or broil 4 in. from the heat for 4-6 minutes on each side or until a thermometer reads 170°.
4. Cut remaining tomatoes in half; grill or broil for 2-3 minutes on each side or until tender. Serve with chicken and reserved dressing.

Nutrition Info:
- 174 cal., 5 g fat (1 g sat. fat), 63 mg chol., 179 mg sodium, 7 g carb., 1 g fiber, 24 g pro.

Chapter 6. Fish & Seafood Recipes

Shrimp And Noodles Parmesan

Servings: 4
Cooking Time:10 Minutes
Ingredients:
- 8 ounces uncooked whole-wheat no-yolk egg noodles
- 1 pound peeled raw shrimp, rinsed and patted dry
- 1/4 cup no-trans-fat margarine (35% vegetable oil)
- 1/4 teaspoon salt
- 3 tablespoons grated fresh Parmesan cheese

Directions:
1. Cook noodles according to package directions, omitting any salt or fat.
2. Meanwhile, place a large nonstick skillet over medium heat until hot. Coat with nonstick cooking spray and sauté the shrimp for 4–5 minutes or until opaque in the center, stirring frequently.
3. Drain the noodles well in a colander and place in a pasta bowl. Add the margarine, shrimp, salt, and black pepper, to taste (if desired), and toss gently. Sprinkle evenly with the Parmesan cheese.

Nutrition Info:
- 340 cal., 7g fat (1g sag. fat), 190mg chol, 410mg sod., 42g carb (0g sugars, 6g fiber), 33g pro.

Salmon With Lemon-thyme Slices

Servings: 4
Cooking Time:10–12 Minutes
Ingredients:

- 2 medium lemons
- 4 (4-ounce) salmon filets, rinsed and patted dry, skinned (if desired)
- 1/2 teaspoon dried thyme, crushed
- 1/4 teaspoon salt
- 1/4 teaspoon black pepper

Directions:

1. Preheat the oven to 400°F.
2. Line a baking sheet with foil and coat with nonstick cooking spray. Slice one of the lemons into 8 rounds and arrange on the baking sheet.
3. Place the salmon on top of the lemon slices, spray the salmon lightly with nonstick cooking spray, and sprinkle evenly with the thyme, salt, and pepper. Bake the salmon 10–12 minutes or until it flakes with a fork.
4. Cut the other lemon in quarters and squeeze lemon juice evenly over all.

Nutrition Info:

- 180 cal., 9g fat (1g sag. fat), 60mg chol, 220mg sod., 3g carb (1g sugars, 1g fiber), 22g pro.

Pan-seared Sesame-crusted Tuna Steaks

Servings:4
Cooking Time:8 Minutes
Ingredients:

- ¾ cup sesame seeds
- 4 (6-ounce) skinless tuna steaks, 1 inch thick
- 2 tablespoons canola oil
- ¼ teaspoon salt
- ⅛ teaspoon pepper

Directions:

1. Spread sesame seeds in shallow baking dish. Pat tuna steaks dry with paper towels, rub steaks all over with 1 tablespoon oil, then sprinkle with salt and pepper. Press both sides of each steak in sesame seeds to coat.
2. Heat remaining 1 tablespoon oil in 12-inch nonstick skillet over medium-high heat until just smoking. Place steaks in skillet and cook until seeds are golden and tuna is translucent red at center when checked with tip of paring knife and registers 110 degrees (for rare), 1 to 2 minutes per side. Transfer tuna to cutting board and slice ½ inch thick. Serve.

Nutrition Info:

- 330 cal., 15g fat (1g sag. fat), 65mg chol, 250mg sod., 2g carb (0g sugars, 1g fiber), 45g pro.

Sautéed Sole

Servings:4
Cooking Time:x
Ingredients:

- ½ cup all-purpose flour
- 8 (2-ounce) skinless sole fillets, ¼ to ½ inch thick
- ¼ teaspoon salt
- ⅛ teaspoon pepper
- ¼ cup extra-virgin olive oil
- Lemon wedges

Directions:

1. Place flour in shallow dish. Pat sole dry with paper towels and sprinkle with salt and pepper. Working with 1 fillet at a time, dredge in flour to coat, shaking off any excess.
2. Heat 2 tablespoons oil in 12-inch nonstick skillet over medium-high heat until shimmering. Place half of sole in skillet and cook until lightly browned on first side, 2 to 3 minutes. Gently flip sole using 2 spatulas and continue to cook until sole flakes apart when gently prodded with paring knife, 30 to 60 seconds.
3. Transfer sole to serving platter and tent loosely with aluminum foil. Wipe skillet clean with paper towels and repeat with remaining 2 tablespoons oil and fillets. Serve with lemon wedges.

Nutrition Info:

- 220 cal., 16g fat (2g sag. fat), 50mg chol, 240mg sod., 3g carb (0g sugars, 0g fiber), 14g pro.

Teriyaki Salmon

Servings:4
Cooking Time: 30 Minutes
Ingredients:

- 3/4 cup reduced-sodium teriyaki sauce
- 1/2 cup maple syrup
- 4 salmon fillets (6 ounces each)
- Mixed salad greens, optional

Directions:

1. In a small bowl, whisk teriyaki sauce and syrup. Pour 1 cup marinade into a large resealable plastic bag. Add salmon; seal bag and turn to coat. Refrigerate 15 minutes. Cover and refrigerate any of the remaining marinade.
2. Drain the salmon, discarding the marinade in bag. Moisten a paper towel with cooking oil; using long-handled tongs, rub on grill rack to coat lightly.
3. Place salmon on grill rack, skin side down. Grill, covered, over medium heat or broil 4 in. from heat 8-12 minutes or until fish just begins to flake easily with a fork, basting frequently with reserved marinade. If desired, serve over mixed salad greens.

Nutrition Info:

- 362 cal., 18g fat (4g sat. fat), 100mg chol., 422mg sod., 12g carb. (12g sugars, 0 fiber), 35g pro.

Lemon-pepper Halibut And Squash Packets

Servings: 4
Cooking Time: 30 Minutes
Ingredients:

- 1 lb halibut fillets (½ to ¾ inch thick)
- 2 teaspoons dried basil leaves
- 1 teaspoon lemon-pepper seasoning
- 1 teaspoon seasoned salt
- 3 medium zucchini or yellow summer squash, cut into 2 × 1-inch strips
- 1 medium red bell pepper, cut into 1-inch pieces
- 2 tablespoons olive or canola oil

Directions:

1. Heat gas or charcoal grill. Cut 4 (18 × 12-inch) sheets of heavy-duty foil; spray with cooking spray. Cut halibut into 4 serving pieces if necessary. Place 1 fish piece on center of each sheet. Sprinkle fillets with 1 teaspoon of the basil, ½ teaspoon of the lemon-pepper seasoning and ½ teaspoon of the seasoned salt. Arrange zucchini and bell pepper evenly over fish. Sprinkle with remaining basil, lemon-pepper seasoning and seasoned salt. Drizzle with oil.
2. Bring up 2 sides of foil over fish and vegetables so edges meet. Seal edges, making tight ½-inch fold; fold again, allowing space for heat circulation and expansion. Fold other sides to seal.
3. Place packets on grill over medium heat. Cover grill; cook 15 to 20 minutes, rotating packets ½ turn after 8 minutes, until fish flakes easily with fork and vegetables are tender. To serve, cut large X across top of each packet; carefully fold back foil to allow steam to escape.

Nutrition Info:

- 200 cal., 9g fat (1.5g sat. fat), 60 chol., 540mg sod., 7g carb. (4g sugars, 2g fiber), 24g pro.

Parmesan Fish Fillets

Servings: 2
Cooking Time: 30 Minutes
Ingredients:

- 1/4 cup egg substitute
- 1 tablespoon fat-free milk
- 1/3 cup grated Parmesan cheese
- 2 tablespoons all-purpose flour
- 2 tilapia fillets (5 ounces each)

Directions:

1. In a shallow bowl, combine egg substitute and milk. In another shallow bowl, combine cheese and flour. Dip fillets in egg mixture, then coat with cheese mixture.
2. Place on a baking sheet coated with cooking spray. Bake at 350° for 20-25 minutes or until the fish flakes easily with a fork.

Nutrition Info:

- 196 cal., 5 g fat (3 g sat. fat), 78 mg chol., 279 mg sodium, 5 g carb., trace fiber, 33 g pro.

Grilled Salmon Packets

Servings: 4
Cooking Time: 25 Minutes
Ingredients:

- 4 salmon fillets (6 ounces each)
- 3 cups fresh sugar snap peas
- 1 small sweet red pepper, cut into strips
- 1 small sweet yellow pepper, cut into strips
- 1/4 cup reduced-fat Asian toasted sesame salad dressing

Directions:

1. Place each salmon fillet on a double thickness of heavy-duty foil (about 12 in. square). Combine sugar snap peas and peppers; spoon over salmon. Drizzle with salad dressing. Fold foil around mixture and seal tightly.
2. Grill, covered, over medium heat for 15-20 minutes or until fish flakes easily with a fork. Open foil carefully to allow steam to escape.

Nutrition Info:

- 350 cal., 17 g fat (3 g sat. fat), 85 mg chol., 237 mg sodium, 14 g carb., 4 g fiber, 34 g pro.

Two-sauce Cajun Fish

Servings: 4
Cooking Time:12–15 Minutes
Ingredients:

- 4 (4-ounce) tilapia filets (or any mild, lean white fish filets), rinsed and patted dry
- 1/2 teaspoon seafood seasoning
- 1 (14.5-ounce) can stewed tomatoes with Cajun seasonings, well drained
- 2 tablespoons no-trans-fat margarine (35% vegetable oil)

Directions:

1. Preheat the oven to 400°F.
2. Coat a broiler rack and pan with nonstick cooking spray, arrange the fish filets on the rack about 2 inches apart, and sprinkle them evenly with the seafood seasoning.
3. Place the tomatoes in a blender and puree until just smooth. Set aside 1/4 cup of the mixture in a small glass bowl.
4. Spoon the remaining tomatoes evenly over the top of each filet and bake 12–15 minutes or until the filets are opaque in the center.
5. Meanwhile, add the margarine to the reserved 1/4 cup tomato mixture and microwave on HIGH 20 seconds or until the mixture is just melted. Stir to blend well.
6. Place the filets on a serving platter, spoon the tomato-margarine mixture over the center of each filet, and sprinkle each lightly with chopped fresh parsley, if desired.

Nutrition Info:

- 150 cal., 5g fat (1g sag. fat), 50mg chol, 250mg sod., 4g carb (3g sugars, 1g fiber), 23g pro.

Pesto Grilled Salmon

Servings:12
Cooking Time: 30 Minutes
Ingredients:
- 1 salmon fillet (3 pounds)
- 1/2 cup prepared pesto
- 2 green onions, finely chopped
- 1/4 cup lemon juice
- 2 garlic cloves, minced

Directions:
1. Moisten a paper towel with cooking oil; using long-handled tongs, lightly coat the grill rack. Place salmon skin side down on grill rack. Grill, covered, over medium heat or broil 4 in. from the heat for 5 minutes.
2. In a small bowl, combine the pesto, onions, lemon juice and garlic. Carefully spoon some of the pesto mixture over salmon. Grill for about15-20 minutes longer or until the fish flakes easily with a fork, basting occasionally with the remaining pesto mixture.

Nutrition Info:
- 262 cal., 17g fat (4g sat. fat), 70mg chol., 147mg sod., 1g carb. (0 sugars, 0 fiber), 25g pro.

Lemony Steamed Spa Fish

Servings:4
Cooking Time:6 Minutes
Ingredients:
- 2 lemons, sliced into ¼-inch-thick rounds, plus lemon wedges for serving
- 4 (6-ounce) sole fillets, ¼ to ½ inch thick
- ¼ teaspoon salt
- ⅛ teaspoon pepper
- 1 tablespoon minced fresh chives, tarragon, cilantro, basil, or parsley

Directions:
1. Place steamer basket in Dutch oven and add water until it just touches bottom of basket. Line basket with half of lemon slices, cover pot, and bring water to boil over high heat. Meanwhile, pat sole dry with paper towels, sprinkle with salt and pepper, and roll each fillet into bundle.
2. Reduce heat to medium-low and bring water to simmer. Lay fish bundles in basket, seam-side down, and top with remaining lemon slices. Cover pot and steam until sole flakes apart when gently prodded with paring knife, 4 to 6 minutes.
3. Gently transfer fish bundles to individual serving plates (discarding lemon slices), sprinkle with herbs, and serve with lemon wedges.

Nutrition Info:
- 120 cal., 3g fat (1g sag. fat), 75mg chol, 280mg sod., 0g carb (0g sugars, 0g fiber), 21g pro.

Baked Italian Tilapia

Servings: 4
Cooking Time: 50 Minutes
Ingredients:

- 4 tilapia fillets (6 ounces each)
- 1/4 teaspoon pepper
- 1 can (14 1/2 ounces) diced tomatoes with basil, oregano and garlic, drained
- 1 large onion, halved and thinly sliced
- 1 medium green pepper, julienned
- 1/4 cup shredded Parmesan cheese

Directions:

1. Place tilapia in a 13-in. x 9-in. baking dish coated with cooking spray, sprinkle with pepper. Spoon the tomatoes over tilapia; top with onion and green pepper.
2. Cover and bake at 350° for 30 minutes. Uncover; sprinkle with cheese. Bake 10-15 minutes longer or until fish flakes easily with a fork.

Nutrition Info:

- 215 cal., 4 g fat (2 g sat. fat), 86 mg chol., 645 mg sodium, 12 g carb., 2 g fiber, 36 g pro.

Buttery Lemon Grilled Fish On Grilled Asparagus

Servings: 4
Cooking Time:12 Minutes
Ingredients:

- 1 pound asparagus spears, ends trimmed
- 4 (4-ounce) cod filets, rinsed and patted dry
- Juice and zest of a medium lemon
- 1/4 cup light butter with canola oil

Directions:

1. Heat a grill or grill pan over medium-high heat. Coat the asparagus with cooking spray and cook 6–8 minutes or until just tender-crisp, turning occasionally. Set aside on a rimmed serving platter and cover to keep warm.
2. Coat both sides of the fish with cooking spray, sprinkle with 1/4 teaspoon black pepper, if desired, and cook 3 minutes on each side or until opaque in center.
3. Meanwhile, combine the light butter, lemon zest and 1/4 teaspoon salt, if desired, in a small bowl.
4. Spoon the butter mixture over the asparagus and spread over all. Top with the fish and squeeze lemon juice over fish.

Nutrition Info:

- 160 cal., 6g fat (1g sag. fat), 50mg chol, 210mg sod., 6g carb (3g sugars, 3g fiber), 23g pro.

Italian-style Tilapia Fillets

Servings: 4
Cooking Time: 15 Minutes
Ingredients:

- 1 lb tilapia or catfish fillets, cut into 4 serving pieces
- 1 teaspoon salt-free seasoning blend
- 1 tablespoon olive or canola oil
- 1 clove garlic, finely chopped
- 1 pint (2 cups) cherry tomatoes, cut in half
- ¼ cup sliced ripe olives, drained

Directions:

1. Sprinkle both sides of fish fillets with seasoning blend. In 12-inch nonstick skillet, heat oil over medium-high heat. Add fish; cook 6 to 8 minutes, turning once, until golden. Remove fish from skillet; cover to keep warm.
2. Heat same skillet over medium-high heat. Add garlic; cook and stir 30 seconds. Add tomatoes; cook about 3 minutes, stirring occasionally, until softened and juicy. Stir in olives. Serve over fish.

Nutrition Info:

- 160 cal., 6g fat (1g sat. fat), 60 chol., 170mg sod., 4g carb. (2g sugars, 1g fiber), 22g pro.

No-fry Fish Fry

Servings: 4
Cooking Time:6 Minutes
Ingredients:

- 2 tablespoons yellow cornmeal
- 2 teaspoons Cajun seasoning
- 4 (4-ounce) tilapia filets (or any mild, lean white fish filets), rinsed and patted dry
- 1/8 teaspoon salt
- Lemon wedges (optional)

Directions:

1. Preheat the broiler.
2. Coat a broiler rack and pan with nonstick cooking spray and set aside.
3. Mix the cornmeal and Cajun seasoning thoroughly in a shallow pan, such as a pie plate. Coat each filet with nonstick cooking spray and coat evenly with the cornmeal mixture.
4. Place the filets on the rack and broil 6 inches away from the heat source for 3 minutes on each side.
5. Place the filets on a serving platter, sprinkle each evenly with salt, and serve with lemon wedges, if desired.

Nutrition Info:

- 130 cal., 2g fat (0g sag. fat), 50mg chol, 250mg sod., 4g carb (0g sugars, 0g fiber), 23g pro.

Salmon With Lemon-dill Butter

Servings: 2
Cooking Time: 15 Minutes
Ingredients:
- 2 salmon fillets (4 ounces each)
- 5 teaspoons reduced-fat butter, melted
- 3/4 teaspoon lemon juice
- 1/2 teaspoon grated lemon peel
- 1/2 teaspoon snipped fresh dill

Directions:
1. Place salmon skin side down on a broiler pan. Combine the butter, lemon juice, lemon peel and dill. Brush one-third of mixture over salmon. Broil 3-4 in. from the heat for 7-9 minutes or until fish flakes easily with a fork, basting occasionally with remaining butter mixture.

Nutrition Info:
- 219 cal., 15 g fat (5 g sat. fat), 69 mg chol., 136 mg sodium, 1 g carb., trace fiber, 19 g pro.

Oven-roasted Salmon

Servings:4
Cooking Time:10 Minutes
Ingredients:
- 1 (1½-pound) skin-on salmon fillet, 1 inch thick
- 1 teaspoon extra-virgin olive oil
- ¼ teaspoon salt
- ⅛ teaspoon pepper

Directions:
1. Adjust oven rack to lowest position, place aluminum foil–lined rimmed baking sheet on rack, and heat oven to 500 degrees. Cut salmon crosswise into 4 fillets, then make 4 or 5 shallow slashes about an inch apart along skin side of each piece, being careful not to cut into flesh. Pat fillets dry with paper towels, rub with oil, and sprinkle with salt and pepper.
2. Once oven reaches 500 degrees, reduce oven temperature to 275 degrees. Remove sheet from oven and carefully place salmon, skin-side down, on hot sheet. Roast until centers are still translucent when checked with tip of paring knife and register 125 degrees (for medium-rare), 4 to 6 minutes.
3. Slide spatula along underside of fillets and transfer to individual serving plates or serving platter, leaving skin behind; discard skin. Serve.

Nutrition Info:
- 360 cal., 24g fat (5g sag. fat), 95mg chol, 250mg sod., 0g carb (0g sugars, 0g fiber), 35g pro.

Chapter 7. Special Treats

Banana-pineapple Cream Pies

Servings:2
Cooking Time: 15 Minutes
Ingredients:
- 1/4 cup cornstarch
- 1/4 cup sugar
- 1 can (20 ounces) unsweetened crushed pineapple, undrained
- 3 medium bananas, sliced
- Two 9-inch graham cracker crusts (about 6 ounces each)
- 1 carton (8 ounces) frozen whipped topping, thawed

Directions:
1. In a large saucepan, combine cornstarch and sugar. Stir in pineapple until blended. Bring to a boil; cook and stir 1-2 minutes or until thickened.
2. Arrange bananas over bottom of each crust; spread the pineapple mixture over tops. Refrigerate at least 1 hour before serving. Top with the whipped topping.

Nutrition Info:
- 205 cal., 8g fat (3g sat. fat), 0 chol., 122mg sod., 33g carb. (23g sugars, 1g fiber), 1g pro.

Strawberry Mousse

Servings:8
Cooking Time:x
Ingredients:
- 2 pounds strawberries, hulled (6½ cups)
- ¼ cup (1¾ ounces) sugar
- Pinch salt
- 1¾ teaspoons unflavored gelatin
- 4 ounces cream cheese, cut into 8 pieces and softened
- ½ cup heavy cream

Directions:
1. Dice enough strawberries into ¼-inch pieces to measure 1 cup; refrigerate until serving. Pulse remaining strawberries in food processor in 2 batches until most pieces are ¼ to ½ inch thick, 6 to 10 pulses. Combine processed strawberries, sugar, and salt in bowl. Cover and let strawberries sit, stirring occasionally, for 45 minutes. (Do not clean processor.)
2. Drain processed strawberries in fine-mesh strainer set over bowl (you should have about ⅔ cup juice). Measure out 3 tablespoons juice into small bowl, sprinkle gelatin over top, and let sit until gelatin softens, about 5 minutes. Place remaining juice in small saucepan and cook over medium-high heat until reduced to 3 tablespoons, about 10 minutes. Remove pan from heat, add softened gelatin mixture, and whisk until dissolved. Add cream cheese and whisk until smooth. Transfer mixture to large bowl.
3. While juice is reducing, return drained strawberries to now-empty processor and process until smooth, 15 to 20 seconds. Strain puree through fine-mesh strainer into medium bowl, pressing on solids to remove seeds and pulp (you should have about 1⅔ cups puree). Discard remaining solids. Add strawberry puree to juice-gelatin mixture and whisk until incorporated.
4. Using stand mixer fitted with whisk attachment, whip cream on medium-low speed until foamy, about 1 minute. Increase speed to high and whip until stiff peaks form, 1 to 3 minutes. Add whipped cream to strawberry mixture and whisk until no white streaks remain. Portion evenly into 8 dessert dishes and chill for at least 4 hours or up to 2 days. (If chilled longer than 6 hours, let mousse sit at room temperature for 15 minutes before serving.) Garnish with reserved diced strawberries and serve.

Nutrition Info:
- 160 cal., 10g fat (6g sag. fat), 35mg chol, 75mg sod., 16g carb (12g sugars, 2g fiber), 3g pro.

Strawberries With Balsamic Vinegar

Servings:6
Cooking Time:x
Ingredients:

- ⅓ cup balsamic vinegar
- 2 teaspoons granulated sugar
- ½ teaspoon lemon juice
- 2 pounds strawberries, hulled and sliced lengthwise ¼ inch thick (5 cups)
- 1 tablespoon packed light brown sugar
- Pinch pepper

Directions:

1. Bring vinegar, granulated sugar, and lemon juice to simmer in small saucepan over medium heat and cook, stirring occasionally, until thickened and measures about 3 tablespoons, about 3 minutes. Transfer syrup to small bowl and let cool completely.
2. Gently toss strawberries with brown sugar and pepper in large bowl. Let sit at room temperature, stirring occasionally, until strawberries begin to release their juice, 10 to 15 minutes. Pour syrup over strawberries and gently toss to combine. Serve.

Nutrition Info:

- 80 cal., 0g fat (0g sag. fat), 0mg chol, 0mg sod., 19g carb (15g sugars, 3g fiber), 1g pro.

Pomegranate And Nut Chocolate Clusters

Servings:12
Cooking Time: 30 Minutes
Ingredients:

- ⅓ cup pecans, toasted and chopped
- ¼ cup shelled pistachios, toasted and chopped
- 2 tablespoons unsweetened flaked coconut, toasted
- 2 tablespoons pomegranate seeds
- 3 ounces semisweet chocolate, chopped fine

Directions:

1. Line rimmed baking sheet with parchment paper. Combine pecans, pistachios, coconut, and pomegranate seeds in bowl.
2. Microwave 2 ounces chocolate in bowl at 50 percent power, stirring often, until about two-thirds melted, 45 to 60 seconds. Remove bowl from microwave; stir in remaining 1 ounce chocolate until melted. If necessary, microwave chocolate at 50 percent power for 5 seconds at a time until melted.
3. Working quickly, measure 1 teaspoon melted chocolate onto prepared sheet and spread into 2½-inch wide circle using back of spoon. Repeat with remaining chocolate, spacing circles 1½ inches apart.
4. Sprinkle pecan mixture evenly over chocolate and press gently to adhere. Refrigerate until chocolate is firm, about 30 minutes. Serve.

Nutrition Info:

- 80 cal., 6g fat (2g sag. fat), 0mg chol, 0mg sod., 6g carb (5g sugars, 1g fiber), 1g pro.

Frozen Chocolate Monkey Treats

Servings:1
Cooking Time: 20 Minutes
Ingredients:

- 3 medium bananas
- 1 cup (6 ounces) dark chocolate chips
- 2 teaspoons shortening
- Toppings: chopped peanuts, toasted flaked coconut and/or colored jimmies

Directions:
1. Cut each banana into six pieces (about 1 in.). Insert a toothpick into each piece; transfer to a waxed paper-lined baking sheet. Freeze until completely firm, about 1 hour.
2. In a microwave, melt chocolate and shortening; stir until smooth. Dip banana pieces in chocolate mixture; allow excess to drip off. Dip in toppings as desired; return to baking sheet. Freeze 30 minutes before serving.

Nutrition Info:

- 72 cal., 4g fat (2g sat. fat), 0 chol., 0 sod., 10g carb. (7g sugars, 1g fiber), 1g pro.

Raspberry-banana Soft Serve

Servings:2
Cooking Time: 10 Minutes
Ingredients:

- 4 medium ripe bananas
- 1/2 cup fat-free plain yogurt
- 1 to 2 tablespoons maple syrup
- 1/2 cup frozen unsweetened raspberries
- Fresh raspberries, optional

Directions:
1. Thinly slice bananas; transfer to a large resealable plastic freezer bag. Arrange slices in a single layer; freeze overnight.
2. Pulse bananas in a food processor until finely chopped. Add yogurt, maple syrup and raspberries. Process just until smooth, scraping sides as needed. Serve immediately, adding fresh berries if desired.

Nutrition Info:

- 104 cal., 0 fat (0 sat. fat), 1mg chol., 15mg sod., 26g carb. (15g sugars, 2g fiber), 2g pro.

Frozen Yogurt Fruit Pops

Servings:1
Cooking Time: 15 Minutes
Ingredients:

- 2 1/4 cups (18 ounces) raspberry yogurt
- 2 tablespoons lemon juice
- 2 medium ripe bananas, cut into chunks
- 12 freezer pop molds or 12 paper cups (3 ounces each) and wooden pop sticks

Directions:
1. Place the yogurt, lemon juice and bananas in a blender; cover and process until smooth, stopping to stir mixture if necessary.
2. Pour mixture into molds or paper cups. Top molds with holders. If using cups, top with foil and insert sticks through foil. Freeze until firm.
Nutrition Info:

- 60 cal., 1g fat (0 sat. fat), 2mg chol., 23mg sod., 13g carb. (10g sugars, 1g fiber), 2g pro.

Warm Figs With Goat Cheese And Honey

Servings:6
Cooking Time:4 Minutes
Ingredients:

- 2 ounces goat cheese
- 9 fresh figs, halved lengthwise
- 18 walnut halves, toasted
- 2 tablespoons honey

Directions:

1. Adjust oven rack to middle position and heat oven to 500 degrees. Spoon heaping ½ teaspoon goat cheese onto each fig half and arrange on parchment paper–lined rimmed baking sheet. Bake figs until heated through, about 4 minutes; transfer to serving platter.
2. Place 1 walnut half on top of each fig half and drizzle with honey. Serve.

Nutrition Info:

- 140 cal., 6g fat (2g sag. fat), 5mg chol, 45mg sod., 21g carb (18g sugars, 3g fiber), 3g pro.

Grilled Angel Food Cake With Strawberries

Servings:8
Cooking Time: 15 Minutes
Ingredients:

- 2 cups sliced fresh strawberries
- 2 teaspoons sugar
- 3 tablespoons butter, melted
- 2 tablespoons balsamic vinegar
- 8 slices angel food cake (about 1 ounce each)
- Reduced-fat vanilla ice cream and blueberries in syrup, optional

Directions:

1. In a bowl, toss strawberries with sugar. In another bowl, mix butter and vinegar; brush over cut sides of cake.
2. On a greased rack, grill cake, uncovered, over medium heat about 1-2 minutes on each side or until golden brown. Serve cake with the strawberries and, if desired, the ice cream and syrup.

Nutrition Info:

- 132 cal., 5g fat (3g sat. fat), 11mg chol., 247mg sod., 22g carb. (4g sugars, 1g fiber), 2g pro.

Fresh Fruit Sauce

Servings:2
Cooking Time: 10 Minutes
Ingredients:

- 1 tablespoon cornstarch
- 1 cup orange juice
- 1/3 cup honey
- 1 cup sliced fresh peaches
- 1 cup sliced fresh plums
- Vanilla ice cream

Directions:

1. In a small saucepan, mix cornstarch and orange juice until smooth; stir in honey. Bring to a boil over medium heat; cook and stir until thickened, about 1 minute.
2. Remove from heat; stir in fruit. Serve warm over ice cream.

Nutrition Info:

- 71 cal., 0 fat (0 sat. fat), 0 chol., 1mg sod., 18g carb. (16g sugars, 1g fiber), 0 pro.

Chapter 8. Salads Recipes

Roasted Asparagus And Strawberry Salad

Servings: 4
Cooking Time: 30 Minutes
Ingredients:
- 1 lb fresh asparagus spears
- Cooking spray
- 4 cups torn mixed salad greens
- 1 cup sliced fresh strawberries
- 2 tablespoons chopped pecans
- ¼ cup balsamic vinaigrette dressing
- Cracked black pepper, if desired

Directions:
1. Heat oven to 400°F. Line 15 × 10 × 1-inch pan with foil; spray with cooking spray. Break off tough ends of asparagus as far down as stalks snap easily. Wash asparagus; cut into 1-inch pieces. Place asparagus in single layer in pan; spray with cooking spray.
2. Bake 10 to 12 minutes or until crisp-tender. Cool completely, about 10 minutes.
3. In medium bowl, mix greens, asparagus, strawberries, pecans and dressing. Sprinkle with pepper.

Nutrition Info:
- 120 cal., 8g fat (0.5g sat. fat), 0 chol., 170mg sod., 10g carb. (6g sugars, 3g fiber), 3g pro.

Lemony Asparagus Spear Salad

Servings: 4
Cooking Time:1 Minute
Ingredients:
- 1 pound asparagus spears, trimmed
- 1 tablespoon basil pesto sauce
- 2 teaspoons lemon juice
- 1/4 teaspoon salt

Directions:
1. Cover asparagus with water in a large skillet and bring to a boil, then cover tightly and cook 1 minute or until tender-crisp.
2. Immediately drain the asparagus in a colander and run under cold water to cool. Place the asparagus on paper towels to drain, then place on a serving platter.
3. Top the asparagus with the pesto and roll the spears back and forth to coat completely. Drizzle with lemon juice and sprinkle with salt. Flavors are at their peak if you serve this within 30 minutes.

Nutrition Info:
- 25 cal., 1g fat (0g sag. fat), 0mg chol, 190mg sod., 3g carb (1g sugars, 1g fiber), 2g pro.

Creamy Dill Cucumbers

Servings: 4
Cooking Time: 6 Minutes
Ingredients:

- 1/4 cup plain fat-free yogurt
- 1 tablespoon reduced-fat mayonnaise
- 1/2 teaspoon dried dill
- 1/4 teaspoon salt
- 2 cups peeled diced cucumber

Directions:

1. Stir the yogurt, mayonnaise, dill, and salt together in a small bowl until completely blended.
2. Place the cucumbers in a medium bowl, add the yogurt mixture, and toss gently to coat completely.
3. Serve within 30 minutes for peak flavors and texture.

Nutrition Info:

- 25 cal., 1g fat (0g sag. fat), 0mg chol, 190mg sod., 3g carb (2g sugars, 0g fiber), 1g pro.

White Bean, Herb And Tomato Salad

Servings: 7
Cooking Time: 30 Minutes
Ingredients:

- 1 can (19 oz) cannellini (white kidney) beans, drained, rinsed
- ¾ cup cubed mozzarella cheese
- 2 tablespoons chopped fresh or 2 teaspoons dried basil leaves
- ⅓ cup fat-free balsamic vinaigrette
- 2 medium tomatoes, chopped (1½ cups)

Directions:

1. In large bowl, mix all ingredients. Serve immediately, or cover and refrigerate 25 minutes before serving.

Nutrition Info:

- 140 cal., 3g fat (2g sat. fat), 10 chol., 200mg sod., 18g carb. (2g sugars, 4g fiber), 10g pro.

Lemon Vinaigrette

Servings:1
Cooking Time:x
Ingredients:

- This vinaigrette is best for dressing mild greens.
- ¼ teaspoon grated lemon zest plus 1 tablespoon juice
- ½ teaspoon mayonnaise
- ½ teaspoon Dijon mustard
- ⅛ teaspoon salt
- Pinch pepper
- 3 tablespoons extra-virgin olive oil

Directions:

1. Whisk lemon zest and juice, mayonnaise, mustard, salt, and pepper together in bowl. While whisking constantly, drizzle in oil until completely emulsified. (Vinaigrette can be refrigerated for up to 1 week; whisk to recombine.)

Nutrition Info:

- 100 cal., 11g fat (1g sag. fat), 0mg chol, 90mg sod., 0g carb (0g sugars, 0g fiber), 0g pro.

Mesclun Salad With Goat Cheese And Almonds

Servings:4
Cooking Time:8minutes
Ingredients:

- 5 ounces (5 cups) mesclun
- 3 tablespoons toasted sliced almonds
- 1 recipe Classic Vinaigrette (this page)
- 2 ounces goat cheese, crumbled (½ cup)

Directions:
1. Gently toss mesclun with almonds and vinaigrette in bowl until well coated. Sprinkle with goat cheese. Serve.

Nutrition Info:
- 170 cal., 16g fat (4g sag. fat), 5mg chol, 160mg sod., 1g carb (0g sugars, 1g fiber), 4g pro.

Toasted Pecan And Apple Salad

Servings: 4
Cooking Time: 8 Minutes
Ingredients:

- 2 tablespoons pecan chips
- 2 cups chopped unpeeled red apples
- 1/4 cup dried raisin-cherry blend (or 1/4 cup dried cherries or golden raisins alone)
- 1 teaspoon honey (or 1 teaspoon packed dark brown sugar and 1 teaspoon water)

Directions:
1. Place a small skillet over medium-high heat until hot. Add the pecans and cook 1–2 minutes or until beginning to lightly brown, stirring constantly. Remove from the heat and set aside on paper towels to stop the cooking process and cool quickly.
2. Combine the apples and dried fruit in a medium bowl, drizzle honey over all, and toss gently.
3. Serve on a lettuce leaf (if desired) or a pretty salad plate. Sprinkle each serving evenly with the pecans.

Nutrition Info:
- 90 cal., 2g fat (0g sag. fat), 0mg chol, 0mg sod., 18g carb (14g sugars, 2g fiber), 1g pro.

Feta'd Tuna With Greens

Servings: 4
Cooking Time: 6 Minutes
Ingredients:

- 6 cups torn Boston Bibb lettuce, red leaf lettuce, or spring greens
- 3 tablespoons fat-free Caesar salad dressing
- 2 ounces crumbled, reduced-fat, sun-dried tomato and basil feta cheese
- 1 (6.4-ounce) packet tuna, broken in large chunks

Directions:
1. Place the lettuce and salad dressing in a large bowl and toss gently, yet thoroughly, to coat completely.
2. Place 1 1/2 cups of lettuce on each of 4 salad plates. Sprinkle each salad with 1 tablespoon feta and lightly flake equal amounts of tuna in the center of each serving. If desired, add a small amount of dressing (such as fat-free Caesar) to the lettuce.

Nutrition Info:
- 80 cal., 2g fat (1g sag. fat), 25mg chol, 360mg sod., 3g carb (1g sugars, 2g fiber), 15g pro.

Orange Pomegranate Salad With Honey

Servings:6
Cooking Time: 15 Minutes
Ingredients:

- 5 medium oranges or 10 clementines
- 1/2 cup pomegranate seeds
- 2 tablespoons honey
- 1 to 2 teaspoons orange flower water or orange juice

Directions:

1. Cut a thin slice from the top and bottom of each orange; stand orange upright on a cutting board. With a knife, cut off peel and outer membrane from oranges. Cut crosswise into 1/2-in. slices.
2. Arrange orange slices on a serving platter; sprinkle with pomegranate seeds. In a small bowl, mix honey and orange flower water; drizzle over fruit.

Nutrition Info:

- 62 cal., 0 fat (0 sat. fat), 0 chol., 2mg sod., 15g carb. (14g sugars, 0 fiber), 1g pro.

Ginger'd Ambrosia

Servings: 4
Cooking Time:5–10 Minutes
Ingredients:

- 3 medium navel oranges, peeled and cut into bite-sized sections (about 1 1/2 cups total)
- 3 tablespoons flaked, sweetened, shredded coconut
- 2–3 teaspoons grated gingerroot
- 4 fresh or canned pineapple slices, packed in juice, drained

Directions:

1. Place all ingredients except the pineapple in a medium bowl and toss gently. If desired, add 1 teaspoon pourable sugar substitute. Let stand 5–10 minutes to develop flavors.
2. Arrange each pineapple slice on a salad plate and spoon a rounded 1/3 cup of the orange mixture on each slice.

Nutrition Info:

- 80 cal., 1g fat (1g sag. fat), 0mg chol, 10mg sod., 18g carb (14g sugars, 3g fiber), 1g pro.

Sausage Spinach Salad

Servings: 2
Cooking Time: 20 Minutes
Ingredients:

- 4 teaspoons olive oil, divided
- 2 fully cooked Italian chicken sausage links (3 ounces each), cut into 1/4-inch slices
- 1/2 medium onion, halved and sliced
- 4 cups fresh baby spinach
- 1 1/2 teaspoons balsamic vinegar
- 1 teaspoon stone-ground mustard

Directions:

1. In a large nonstick skillet coated with cooking spray, heat 1 teaspoon oil over medium heat. Add the sausage and onion; cook and stir until sausage is lightly browned and the onion is crisp-tender.
2. Place spinach in a large bowl. In a small bowl, whisk vinegar, mustard and remaining oil. Drizzle over spinach; toss to coat. Add sausage mixture; serve immediately.

Nutrition Info:

- 244 cal., 16 g fat (3 g sat. fat), 65 mg chol., 581 mg sodium, 8 g carb., 2 g fiber, 17 g pro.

Artichoke Tomato Toss

Servings: 4
Cooking Time: 4 Minutes
Ingredients:

- 1/2 of a 14-ounce can quartered artichoke hearts, drained
- 1 cup grape tomatoes, halved
- 1 tablespoons fat-free Caesar or Italian dressing
- 1 ounce crumbled, reduced-fat, sun-dried tomato and basil feta cheese
- 2 tablespoons chopped fresh parsley (optional)

Directions:
1. In a medium bowl, toss the artichoke hearts, tomatoes, and dressing gently, yet thoroughly. Add the feta and toss gently again.
2. Serve immediately or cover with plastic wrap and refrigerate up to 3 days.

Nutrition Info:

- 45 cal., 1g fat (0g sag. fat), 5mg chol, 270mg sod., 6g carb (2g sugars, 3g fiber), 3g pro.

Thousand Isle Wedges

Servings: 4
Cooking Time: 5 Minutes
Ingredients:

- 3 tablespoons no-salt ketchup
- 1/8 teaspoon salt
- 1 tablespoon reduced-fat mayonnaise
- 1/3 cup fat-free buttermilk
- 1/2 small head iceberg lettuce, cut in 4 wedges

Directions:
1. Stir the ketchup, salt, and mayonnaise together in a small bowl until smooth. Add the buttermilk and blend thoroughly.
2. Place a lettuce wedge on each salad plate, spoon 2 tablespoons dressing on top of each wedge, and sprinkle evenly with black pepper, if desired.

Nutrition Info:

- 40 cal., 1g fat (0g sag. fat), 0mg chol, 125mg sod., 6g carb (5g sugars, 1g fiber), 1g pro.

Caesar'd Chicken Salad

Servings: 4
Cooking Time: 5 Minutes
Ingredients:

- 1/4 cup fat-free mayonnaise
- 3 tablespoons fat-free Caesar salad dressing
- 2 1/2 cups cooked diced chicken breast
- 1/2 cup finely chopped green onion (green and white parts)

Directions:
1. Stir the mayonnaise and salad dressing together in a medium bowl. Add the chicken, onions, and black pepper, if desired, and stir until well coated.
2. Cover with plastic wrap and refrigerate at least 2 hours to allow flavors to blend. You may refrigerate this salad up to 24 hours before serving.
Nutrition Info:

- 170 cal., 3g fat (1g sag. fat), 75mg chol, 460mg sod., 4g carb (2g sugars, 1g fiber), 28g pro.

Seaside Shrimp Salad

Servings: 4
Cooking Time:5 Minutes
Ingredients:

- 1 1/2 pounds peeled raw fresh or frozen and thawed shrimp
- 2 tablespoons reduced-fat mayonnaise
- 1 1/2 teaspoons seafood seasoning
- 6 tablespoons lemon juice

Directions:

1. Bring water to boil in a large saucepan over high heat. Add the shrimp and return to a boil. Reduce the heat and simmer, uncovered, 2–3 minutes or until the shrimp is opaque in the center.
2. Drain the shrimp in a colander, rinse with cold water for 30 seconds, and pat dry with paper towels. Let stand 10 minutes to cool completely.
3. Place shrimp in a medium bowl with the mayonnaise, seafood seasoning, and lemon juice. Stir gently to coat. Cover with plastic wrap and refrigerate 2 hours. Serve as is or over tomato slices or lettuce leaves.

Nutrition Info:

- 130 cal., 2g fat (0g sag. fat), 205mg chol, 430mg sod., 3g carb (1g sugars, 0g fiber), 26g pro.

Balsamic Bean Salsa Salad

Servings: 4
Cooking Time: 15 Minutes
Ingredients:

- 15-ounce can black beans, rinsed and drained
- 1/2 cup chopped red bell pepper
- 1/4 cup finely chopped red onion
- 2 tablespoons balsamic vinegar

Directions:

1. Toss all ingredients in a medium bowl.
2. Let stand 15 minutes to develop flavors.

Nutrition Info:

- 100 cal., 0g fat (0g sag. fat), 0mg chol, 80mg sod., 18g carb (4g sugars, 6g fiber), 6g pro.

Bacon Onion Potato Salad

Servings: 4
Cooking Time:4 Minutes
Ingredients:

- 12 ounces unpeeled red potatoes, diced (about 3 cups)
- 3 tablespoons reduced-fat ranch salad dressing
- 1/2 cup finely chopped green onion
- 2 tablespoons real bacon bits (not imitation)

Directions:

1. Bring water to boil in a medium saucepan over high heat. Add the potatoes and return to a boil. Reduce the heat, cover tightly, and cook 4 minutes or until just tender when pierced with a fork.
2. Drain the potatoes in a colander and run under cold water until cool, about 30 seconds. Drain well and place in a medium bowl with the remaining ingredients. Toss gently to blend well.
3. Serve immediately or cover with plastic wrap and refrigerate 2 hours for a more blended flavor. To serve, add salt, if desired and toss.

Nutrition Info:

- 110 cal., 3g fat (0g sag. fat), 5mg chol, 250mg sod., 16g carb (2g sugars, 2g fiber), 4g pro.

Romaine Salad With Chickpeas And Feta

Servings:4
Cooking Time:8minutes
Ingredients:

- 3 romaine lettuce hearts (18 ounces), torn into bite-size pieces
- 1 cup canned no-salt-added chickpeas, rinsed
- 1 recipe Balsamic-Mustard Vinaigrette (this page)
- 2 ounces feta cheese, crumbled (½ cup)

Directions:

1. Gently toss lettuce and chickpeas with vinaigrette in bowl until well coated. Sprinkle with feta. Serve.

Nutrition Info:

- 230 cal., 14g fat (3g sag. fat), 15mg chol, 290mg sod., 17g carb (5g sugars, 3g fiber), 7g pro.

Crispy Crunch Coleslaw

Servings: 4
Cooking Time: 7 Minutes
Ingredients:

- 3 cups shredded cabbage mix with carrots and red cabbage
- 1 medium green bell pepper, finely chopped
- 2–3 tablespoons apple cider vinegar
- 2 tablespoons Splenda
- 1/8 teaspoon salt

Directions:

1. Place all ingredients in a large zippered plastic bag, seal tightly, and shake to blend thoroughly.
2. Refrigerate 3 hours before serving to blend flavors. This salad tastes best served the same day you make it.

Nutrition Info:

- 20 cal., 0g fat (0g sag. fat), 0mg chol, 85mg sod., 4g carb (2g sugars, 2g fiber), 0g pro.

Chicken Kale Salad With Fresh Ginger Dressing

Servings: 4
Cooking Time:12 Minutes
Ingredients:

- 1 pound boneless, skinless chicken breast
- 8 cups packed spinach with baby kale greens
- 3/4 cup light raspberry salad dressing, such as Newman's Own
- 2 to 3 teaspoons grated gingerroot

Directions:

1. Heat a grill or grill pan over medium-high heat. Coat the chicken with cooking spray, sprinkle with 1/4 teaspoon salt and 1/4 teaspoon pepper, if desired. Cook 6 minutes on each side or until no longer pink in center. Let cool and thinly slice.
2. Place equal amounts of the greens and chicken on four dinner plates. Whisk together the salad dressing and ginger until well blended. Spoon equal amounts over all.

Nutrition Info:

- 230 cal., 10g fat (1g sag. fat), 85mg chol, 440mg sod., 6g carb (3g sugars, 2g fiber), 28g pro.

Pork And Avocado Salad

Servings: 4
Cooking Time:10 Minutes
Ingredients:

- 1 pound boneless center-cut pork loin chops
- 2 ripe medium avocados, chopped
- 1/4 cup fresh lemon
- 1 cup chopped fresh parsley or cilantro

Directions:

1. Heat a grill pan or large skillet coated with cooking spray over medium-high heat. Cook the pork 4 minutes on each side or until slightly pink in center. Place on cutting board to cool.
2. Chop pork and place in a large bowl with 1/2 teaspoon salt and 1/2 teaspoon pepper, if desired, and remaining ingredients; toss gently until well blended.

Nutrition Info:

- 260 cal., 13g fat (2g sag. fat), 70mg chol, 85mg sod., 8g carb (1g sugars, 5g fiber), 28g pro.

Pear And Bleu Cheese Greens

Servings: 4
Cooking Time: 4 Minutes
Ingredients:

- 6 cups spring greens
- 1 1/3 cups firm pear slices or green apple slices
- 6 tablespoons fat-free raspberry vinaigrette
- 3 tablespoons crumbled reduced-fat bleu cheese

Directions:

1. Place 1 1/2 cups of the greens on each of 4 salad plates. Arrange 1/3 cup pear slices on each serving.
2. Top with 1 1/2 tablespoons dressing and 3/4 tablespoon of the cheese. Serve immediately.

Nutrition Info:

- 80 cal., 1g fat (0g sag. fat), 5mg chol, 230mg sod., 15g carb (11g sugars, 2g fiber), 2g pro.

Cumin'd Salsa Salad

Servings: 4
Cooking Time: 3 Minutes
Ingredients:

- 3/4 cup mild or medium salsa fresca (pico de gallo)
- 2 tablespoons water
- 1/4 teaspoon ground cumin
- 8 cups shredded lettuce
- 20 baked bite-sized multi-grain tortilla chips, coarsely crumbled (1 ounce)

Directions:

1. Stir the salsa, water, and cumin together in a small bowl.
2. Place 2 cups of lettuce on each of 4 salad plates, spoon 3 tablespoons picante mixture over each salad, and top with chips.

Nutrition Info:

- 60 cal., 2g fat (0g sag. fat), 0mg chol, 40mg sod., 9g carb (3g sugars, 2g fiber), 2g pro.

Bibb Lettuce Salad With Endive And Cucumber

Servings:4
Cooking Time:12minutes
Ingredients:

- 12 ounces cherry tomatoes, halved
- 1 head Bibb lettuce (8 ounces), leaves separated and torn into bite-size pieces
- 1 head Belgian endive (4 ounces), cut into ½-inch pieces
- 1 cucumber, peeled, halved lengthwise, seeded, and sliced ¼ inch thick
- 1 recipe Parmesan-Peppercorn Dressing (this page)

Directions:

1. Gently toss lettuce and chickpeas with vinaigrette in bowl until well coated. Sprinkle with feta. Serve.

Nutrition Info:

- 110 cal., 7g fat (1g sag. fat), 5mg chol, 140mg sod., 8g carb (4g sugars, 3g fiber), 4g pro.

Tangy Sweet Carrot Pepper Salad

Servings: 4
Cooking Time:1 Minute
Ingredients:

- 1 1/2 cups peeled sliced carrots (about 1/8-inch thick)
- 2 tablespoons water
- 3/4 cup thinly sliced green bell pepper
- 1/3 cup thinly sliced onion
- 1/4 cup reduced-fat Catalina dressing

Directions:

1. Place carrots and water in a shallow, microwave-safe dish, such as a glass pie plate. Cover with plastic wrap and microwave on HIGH for 1 minute or until carrots are just tender-crisp. Be careful not to overcook them—the carrots should retain some crispness.
2. Immediately place the carrots in a colander and run under cold water about 30 seconds to cool. Shake to drain and place the carrots on paper towels to dry further. Dry the dish.
3. When the carrots are completely cool, return them to the dish, add the remaining ingredients, and toss gently to coat.
4. Serve immediately, or chill 30 minutes for a more blended flavor. Flavors are at their peak if you serve this salad within 30 minutes of adding dressing.

Nutrition Info:

- 60 cal., 0g fat (0g sag. fat), 0mg chol, 200mg sod., 11g carb (7g sugars, 2g fiber), 1g pro.

Minted Carrot Salad

Servings: 4
Cooking Time:1 Minute
Ingredients:

- 3 cups thinly sliced carrots (about 12 ounces total)
- 1 tablespoon extra-virgin olive oil
- 1 tablespoon cider vinegar
- 1/3 cup chopped fresh mint (or basil)

Directions:

1. Bring 4 cups water to a rolling boil in a large saucepan. Add the carrots, return to a rolling boil, and cook 30 seconds. Immediately drain in a colander and run under cold water to cool completely. Drain well.
2. Place carrots in a shallow bowl. Top with remaining ingredients and sprinkle evenly with 1/4 teaspoon salt and 1/4 teaspoon pepper. Serve immediately or cover and refrigerate up to 1 hour before serving.

Nutrition Info:

- 75 cal., 4g fat (0g sag. fat), 0mg chol, 70mg sod., 10g carb (5g sugars, 4g fiber), 1g pro.

Zesty Citrus Melon

Servings: 4
Cooking Time: 5 Minutes
Ingredients:

- 1/4 cup orange juice
- 2–3 tablespoons lemon juice
- 1 teaspoon honey
- 3 cups diced honeydew or cantaloupe melon

Directions:

1. Stir the orange juice, lemon zest (if using), lemon juice, and honey together in a small bowl.
2. Place the melon on a serving plate and pour the juice mixture evenly over all. For peak flavor, serve within 1 hour.

Nutrition Info:

- 60 cal., 0g fat (0g sag. fat), 0mg chol, 25mg sod., 15g carb (13g sugars, 1g fiber), 1g pro.

Broccoli Almond Slaw

Servings: 4
Cooking Time:2 Minutes
Ingredients:
- 2 ounces slivered almonds
- 4 cups broccoli slaw
- 2 tablespoons sugar
- 3 tablespoons white balsamic vinegar

Directions:

1. Heat a skillet over medium-high heat. Add the almonds and cook 2 minutes or until beginning to lightly brown, stirring frequently.
2. Combine the almonds and 1/4 teaspoon salt and 1/4 teaspoon pepper, if desired, with the remaining ingredients in a large bowl. Cover and refrigerate 1 hour before serving.

Nutrition Info:

- 150 cal., 7g fat (0g sag. fat), 0mg chol, 120mg sod., 17g carb (10g sugars, 4g fiber), 6g pro.

Carrot Cranberry Matchstick Salad

Servings: 4
Cooking Time: 5 Minutes
Ingredients:

- 3 cups matchstick carrots
- 1 poblano chili pepper, chopped
- 1/3 cup dried cranberries
- Zest and juice of 1 medium lemon

Directions:

1. Combine the ingredients with 1/8 teaspoon salt in a large bowl. Cover and refrigerate 1 hour before serving.

Nutrition Info:

- 70 cal., 0g fat (0g sag. fat), 0mg chol, 105mg sod., 19g carb (11g sugars, 4g fiber), 1g pro.

Melon And Grape Salad

Servings: 4
Cooking Time: 15 Minutes
Ingredients:
- 1 tablespoon lemon juice
- 1 tablespoon honey
- 1 cup bite-size cubes cantaloupe, honeydew melon or watermelon
- 1 cup halved red or green grapes
- 1 teaspoon slivered fresh mint leaves

Directions:
1. In medium bowl, mix lemon juice and honey. Add melon and grapes; toss gently to coat. Sprinkle with mint.

Nutrition Info:
- 60 cal., 0g fat (0g sat. fat), 0 chol., 10mg sod., 15g carb. (14g sugars, 0g fiber), 0g pro.

Chapter 9. Vegetables, Fruit And Side Dishes

Confetti Corn

Servings:4
Cooking Time: 15 Minutes
Ingredients:
- 1/4 cup chopped carrot
- 1 tablespoon olive oil
- 2 3/4 cups fresh or frozen corn, thawed
- 1/4 cup chopped water chestnuts
- 1/4 cup chopped sweet red pepper

Directions:
1. In a large skillet, saute the carrot in oil until crisp-tender. Stir in the corn, water chestnuts and red pepper; heat until warmed through.

Nutrition Info:
- 140 cal., 4g fat (1g sat. fat), 0 chol., 7mg sod., 26g carb. (3g sugars, 3g fiber), 4g pro.

Lemon-garlic Broccoli With Yellow Peppers

Servings: 6
Cooking Time: 20 Minutes
Ingredients:

- 4 cups fresh broccoli florets (about 10 oz)
- ½ cup bite-size strips yellow bell pepper
- 1 tablespoon olive oil
- 1 clove garlic, finely chopped
- 1 tablespoon water
- 1 teaspoon grated lemon peel
- ¼ teaspoon salt

Directions:

1. In 3-quart saucepan, heat 4 cups water to boiling. Add broccoli; heat to boiling. Boil uncovered 2 minutes.
2. Add bell pepper; boil 1 to 2 minutes or until vegetables are crisp-tender. Drain; remove from saucepan.
3. To same saucepan, add oil and garlic. Cook over medium heat, stirring occasionally, until golden. Stir in 1 tablespoon water, the lemon peel and salt. Return broccoli mixture to saucepan; toss to coat.

Nutrition Info:

- 50 cal., 2.5g fat (0g sat. fat), 0 chol., 120mg sod., 5g carb. (1g sugars, 1g fiber), 2g pro.

Broccoli Piquant

Servings: 4
Cooking Time:7 Minutes
Ingredients:

- 10 ounces fresh broccoli florets
- 1 tablespoon no-trans-fat margarine (35% vegetable oil)
- 1 teaspoon Worcestershire sauce
- 1 teaspoon lemon juice
- 1/4 teaspoon salt

Directions:

1. Steam the broccoli for 6 minutes or until the broccoli is tender-crisp.
2. Meanwhile, microwave the remaining ingredients in a small glass bowl on HIGH for 15 seconds. Stir until smooth.
3. Place the broccoli on a serving platter and drizzle the sauce evenly over all.

Nutrition Info:

- 35 cal., 1g fat (0g sag. fat), 0mg chol, 200mg sod., 4g carb (2g sugars, 2g fiber), 2g pro.

Roasted Beets

Servings:4
Cooking Time:60 Minutes
Ingredients:

- 1½ pounds beets, trimmed
- 1 tablespoon extra-virgin olive oil
- 1 tablespoon sherry vinegar
- 1 tablespoon minced fresh parsley
- Salt and pepper

Directions:

1. Adjust oven rack to middle position and heat oven to 400 degrees. Wrap beets individually in aluminum foil and place on rimmed baking sheet. Roast beets until skewer inserted into center meets little resistance (you will need to unwrap beets to test them), 45 to 60 minutes.
2. Remove beets from oven and slowly open foil packets (being careful of rising steam). When beets are cool enough to handle but still warm, gently rub off skins using paper towels.
3. Slice beets into ½-inch-thick wedges, then toss with oil, vinegar, parsley, and ¼ teaspoon salt. Season with pepper to taste and serve warm or at room temperature. (Beets can be refrigerated for up to 3 days; return to room temperature before serving.)

Nutrition Info:

- 80 cal., 3g fat (0g sag. fat), 0mg chol, 240mg sod., 11g carb (8g sugars, 3g fiber), 2g pro.

Sautéed Snow Peas With Lemon And Parsley

Servings:4
Cooking Time:x
Ingredients:

- 1 tablespoon canola oil
- 1 small shallot, minced
- 1 teaspoon finely grated lemon zest plus 1 teaspoon juice
- 12 ounces snow peas, strings removed
- Salt and pepper
- 1 tablespoon minced fresh parsley

Directions:

1. Combine 1 teaspoon oil, shallot, and lemon zest in bowl. Heat remaining 2 teaspoons oil in 12-inch nonstick skillet over high heat until just smoking. Add snow peas and sprinkle with ¼ teaspoon salt and ⅛ teaspoon pepper. Cook, without stirring, for 30 seconds. Stir briefly, then cook, without stirring, for 30 seconds. Continue to cook, stirring constantly, until peas are crisp-tender, 1 to 2 minutes.
2. Clear center of skillet, add shallot mixture, and cook, mashing mixture into skillet, until fragrant, about 30 seconds. Stir shallot mixture into peas. Stir in lemon juice and parsley and season with pepper to taste. Transfer to bowl and serve.

Nutrition Info:

- 70 cal., 3g fat (0g sag. fat), 0mg chol, 150mg sod., 7g carb (4g sugars, 2g fiber), 2g pro.

Sesame Broccoli

Servings: 6
Cooking Time: 25 Minutes
Ingredients:
- 1 pound fresh broccoli, cut into spears
- 1 tablespoon reduced-sodium soy sauce
- 2 teaspoons olive oil
- 2 teaspoons balsamic vinegar
- 1 1/2 teaspoons honey
- 2 teaspoons sesame seeds, toasted

Directions:
1. Place broccoli in a steamer basket; place in a saucepan over 1 in. of water. Bring to a boil; cover and steam for 10-15 minutes or until crisp-tender. Meanwhile, in a small saucepan, combine the soy sauce, oil, vinegar and honey; cook and stir over medium-low heat until heated through.
2. Transfer broccoli to a serving bowl; drizzle with soy sauce mixture. Sprinkle with sesame seeds.

Nutrition Info:
- 48 cal., 2 g fat (trace sat. fat), 0 chol., 127 mg sodium, 6 g carb., 2 g fiber, 3 g pro.

Sautéed Cabbage With Parsley And Lemon

Servings:6
Cooking Time:x
Ingredients:
- 1 small head green cabbage (1¼ pounds), cored and sliced thin
- 2 tablespoons extra-virgin olive oil
- 1 onion, halved and sliced thin
- Salt and pepper
- ¼ cup chopped fresh parsley
- 1½ teaspoons lemon juice

Directions:
1. Place cabbage in large bowl and cover with cold water. Let sit for 3 minutes; drain well.
2. Heat 1 tablespoon oil in 12-inch nonstick skillet over medium-high heat until shimmering. Add onion and ¼ teaspoon salt and cook until softened and lightly browned, 5 to 7 minutes; transfer to bowl.
3. Heat remaining 1 tablespoon oil in now-empty skillet over medium-high heat until shimmering. Add cabbage and sprinkle with ¼ teaspoon salt and ¼ teaspoon pepper. Cover and cook, without stirring, until cabbage is wilted and lightly browned on bottom, about 3 minutes. Stir and continue to cook, uncovered, until cabbage is crisp-tender and lightly browned in places, about 4 minutes, stirring once halfway through cooking. Off heat, stir in onion, parsley, and lemon juice. Season with pepper to taste and serve.

Nutrition Info:
- 80 cal., 4g fat (0g sag. fat), 0mg chol, 220mg sod., 8g carb (4g sugars, 3g fiber), 1g pro.

Broiled Broccoli Rabe

Servings:4
Cooking Time:x
Ingredients:
- 3 tablespoons extra-virgin olive oil
- 1 pound broccoli rabe
- 1 garlic clove, minced
- ¼ teaspoon salt
- ¼ teaspoon red pepper flakes
- Lemon wedges

Directions:
1. Adjust oven rack 4 inches from broiler element and heat broiler. Brush rimmed baking sheet with 1 tablespoon oil.
2. Trim and discard bottom 1 inch of broccoli rabe stems. Wash broccoli rabe with cold water, then dry with clean dish towel. Cut tops (leaves and florets) from stems, then cut stems into 1-inch pieces (keep tops whole). Transfer broccoli rabe to prepared sheet.
3. Combine remaining 2 tablespoons oil, garlic, salt, and pepper flakes in small bowl. Pour oil mixture over broccoli rabe and toss to combine.
4. Broil until half of leaves are well browned, 2 to 2½ minutes. Using tongs, toss to expose unbrowned leaves. Return sheet to oven and continue to broil until most leaves are lightly charred and stems are crisp-tender, 2 to 2½ minutes. Transfer to serving platter and serve, passing lemon wedges.

Nutrition Info:
- 120 cal., 11g fat (1g sag. fat), 0mg chol, 180mg sod., 4g carb (0g sugars, 3g fiber), 4g pro.

Cran-orange Swiss Chard

Servings: 4
Cooking Time: 25 Minutes
Ingredients:
- 1 medium onion, sliced
- 1 tablespoon olive oil
- 10 cups chopped Swiss chard
- 1/4 cup orange juice
- 2 tablespoons dried cranberries
- Dash salt and pepper
- 2 tablespoons coarsely chopped walnuts, toasted

Directions:
1. In a large skillet, saute onion in oil until tender. Add chard; saute for 3-5 minutes or just until wilted.
2. Stir in the orange juice, cranberries, salt and pepper; cook for 1-2 minutes or until cranberries are softened. Sprinkle with walnuts.

Nutrition Info:
- 104 cal., 6 g fat (1 g sat. fat), 0 chol., 230 mg sodium, 12 g carb., 3 g fiber, 3 g pro.

Hearty Beans And Rice

Servings: 5
Cooking Time: 25 Minutes
Ingredients:
- 1 pound lean ground beef (90% lean)
- 1 can (15 ounces) black beans, rinsed and drained
- 1 can (14 1/2 ounces) diced tomatoes with mild green chilies, undrained
- 1 1/3 cups frozen corn, thawed
- 1 cup water
- 1/4 teaspoon salt
- 1 1/2 cups instant brown rice

Directions:
1. In a large saucepan, cook beef over medium heat until no longer pink; drain. Stir in the beans, tomatoes, corn, water and salt. Bring to a boil. Stir in rice; return to a boil. Reduce heat; cover and simmer for 5 minutes. Remove from the heat; let stand, covered, for 5 minutes.

Nutrition Info:
- 376 cal., 9 g fat (3 g sat. fat), 56 mg chol., 647 mg sodium, 47 g carb., 7 g fiber, 26 g pro.

Green Beans With Roasted Grape Tomatoes

Servings: 10
Cooking Time: 45 Minutes
Ingredients:
- 2 teaspoons olive oil
- 1/4 teaspoon grated lemon peel
- 2 pints grape tomatoes
- 1/4 teaspoon celery salt
- Dash white pepper
- 1 1/2 pounds fresh green beans, trimmed
- 2 tablespoons grated Romano or Parmesan cheese

Directions:
1. In a small bowl, combine oil and lemon peel. Place tomatoes in a greased 15-in. x 10-in. x 1-in. baking pan; drizzle with oil mixture. Sprinkle with celery salt and pepper; toss to coat. Bake at 350° for 35-40 minutes or until very tender, stirring once.
2. Meanwhile, place beans in a steamer basket; place in a saucepan over 1 in. of water. Bring to a boil; cover and steam for 7-8 minutes or until crisp-tender. Transfer to a serving plate.
3. Place tomatoes over the beans; sprinkle with cheese. Serve warm or at room temperature.

Nutrition Info:
- 45 cal., 2 g fat (trace sat. fat), 2 mg chol., 72 mg sodium, 7 g carb., 3 g fiber, 2 g pro.

Grilled Summer Squash

Servings: 4
Cooking Time: 25 Minutes
Ingredients:

- 2 medium yellow summer squash, sliced
- 2 medium sweet red peppers, sliced
- 1 large sweet onion, halved and sliced
- 2 tablespoons olive oil
- 2 garlic cloves, minced
- 1 teaspoon sugar
- 1/4 teaspoon salt
- 1/4 teaspoon pepper

Directions:

1. In a large bowl, combine all the ingredients. Divide between two double thicknesses of heavy-duty foil (about 18 in. x 12 in.). Fold foil around vegetable mixture and seal tightly.
2. Grill, covered, over medium heat for 10-15 minutes or until vegetables are tender. Open foil carefully to allow steam to escape.

Nutrition Info:

- 124 cal., 7 g fat (1 g sat. fat), 0 chol., 159 mg sodium, 15 g carb., 3 g fiber, 3 g pro.

Sautéed Swiss Chard With Garlic

Servings:6
Cooking Time:8 Minutes
Ingredients:

- 2 tablespoons extra-virgin olive oil
- 3 garlic cloves, sliced thin
- 1½ pounds Swiss chard, stems sliced ¼ inch thick on bias, leaves sliced into ½-inch-wide strips
- 2 teaspoons lemon juice
- Pepper

Directions:

1. Heat oil in 12-inch nonstick skillet over medium-high heat until just shimmering. Add garlic and cook, stirring constantly, until lightly browned, 30 to 60 seconds. Add chard stems and cook, stirring occasionally, until spotty brown and crisp-tender, about 6 minutes.
2. Add two-thirds of chard leaves and cook, tossing with tongs, until just starting to wilt, 30 to 60 seconds. Add remaining chard leaves and continue to cook, stirring frequently, until leaves are tender, about 3 minutes. Off heat, stir in lemon juice and season with pepper to taste. Serve.

Nutrition Info:

- 60 cal., 5g fat (0g sag. fat), 0mg chol, 220mg sod., 5g carb (1g sugars, 2g fiber), 2g pro.

Whipped Cauliflower

Servings: 4
Cooking Time: 20 Minutes
Ingredients:

- 1 medium head cauliflower, cut into florets
- 1/4 cup fat-free milk
- 2 tablespoons canola oil
- 1/4 teaspoon salt
- 1/8 teaspoon white pepper

Directions:
1. Place cauliflower in a steamer basket; place in a saucepan over 1 in. of water. Bring to a boil; cover and steam for 8-10 minutes or until tender. Cool cauliflower slightly.
2. Place the milk and oil in a blender. Add the cauliflower, salt and pepper; cover and process until blended. Transfer to a serving bowl.

Nutrition Info:
- 105 cal., 7 g fat (1 g sat. fat), 1 mg chol., 199 mg sodium, 8 g carb., 4 g fiber, 3 g pro.

Creole-simmered Vegetables

Servings: 4
Cooking Time:24 Minutes
Ingredients:

- 1 (14.5-ounce) can stewed tomatoes with Cajun seasonings
- 2 cups frozen pepper and onion stir-fry
- 3/4 cup thinly sliced celery
- 1 tablespoon no-trans-fat margarine (35% vegetable oil)

Directions:
1. Place all the ingredients except the margarine in a medium saucepan and bring to a boil over high heat. Reduce the heat, cover tightly, and simmer 20 minutes or until the onions are very tender.
2. Increase the heat to high and cook 2 minutes, uncovered, to thicken the vegetables slightly. Remove from the heat and stir in the margarine.
Nutrition Info:
- 60 cal., 1g fat (0g sag. fat), 0mg chol, 210mg sod., 10g carb (6g sugars, 2g fiber), 2g pro.

Roasted Spiralized Carrots

Servings:6
Cooking Time:15 Minutes
Ingredients:

- 2 pounds carrots, trimmed and peeled
- 2 tablespoons extra-virgin olive oil
- 2 teaspoons minced fresh thyme
- Salt and pepper

Directions:
1. Adjust oven rack to middle position and heat oven to 375 degrees. Using spiralizer, cut carrots into ⅛-inch-thick noodles, then cut noodles into 12-inch lengths. Toss carrots with 1 tablespoon oil, thyme, ½ teaspoon salt, and ¼ teaspoon pepper on rimmed baking sheet. Cover baking sheet tightly with aluminum foil and roast for 15 minutes. Remove foil and continue to roast until carrots are tender, 10 to 15 minutes.
2. Transfer carrots to serving platter, drizzle with remaining 1 tablespoon oil, and season with pepper to taste. Serve.
Nutrition Info:
- 100 cal., 5g fat (0g sag. fat), 0mg chol, 290mg sod., 13g carb (6g sugars, 4g fiber), 1g pro.

Braised Fennel With White Winc And Parmesan

Servings:4
Cooking Time:25 Minutes
Ingredients:
- 3 tablespoons extra-virgin olive oil
- 2 fennel bulbs, stalks discarded, bulbs cut vertically into ½-inch-thick slices
- Salt and pepper
- ⅓ cup dry white wine
- ¼ cup grated Parmesan cheese

Directions:
1. Heat 2 tablespoons oil in 12-inch nonstick skillet over medium heat until shimmering. Add fennel and sprinkle with ⅛ teaspoon salt and ⅛ teaspoon pepper. Add wine, cover, and simmer for 15 minutes.
2. Turn slices over and continue to simmer, covered, until fennel is nearly tender, has absorbed most of liquid, and starts to turn golden, about 10 minutes.
3. Turn fennel again and continue to cook until golden on second side, about 4 minutes. Transfer to serving platter, drizzle with remaining 1 tablespoon oil, and sprinkle with Parmesan. Serve.

Nutrition Info:
- 160 cal., 12g fat (2g sag. fat), 5mg chol, 200mg sod., 9g carb (5g sugars, 4g fiber), 3g pro.

Roasted Asparagus

Servings:6
Cooking Time:10 Minutes
Ingredients:
- 2 pounds thick asparagus, trimmed
- 2 tablespoons plus 2 teaspoons extra-virgin olive oil
- ½ teaspoon salt
- ¼ teaspoon pepper

Directions:
1. Adjust oven rack to lowest position, place rimmed baking sheet on rack, and heat oven to 500 degrees. Peel bottom halves of asparagus spears until white flesh is exposed, then toss with 2 tablespoons oil, salt, and pepper.
2. Transfer asparagus to preheated sheet and spread into single layer. Roast, without moving asparagus, until undersides of spears are browned, tops are bright green, and tip of paring knife inserted at base of largest spear meets little resistance, 8 to 10 minutes. Transfer asparagus to serving platter and drizzle with remaining 2 teaspoons oil. Serve.

Nutrition Info:
- 80 cal., 6g fat (1g sag. fat), 0mg chol, 190mg sod., 4g carb (2g sugars, 2g fiber), 3g pro.

Slow-cooked Whole Carrots

Servings:6
Cooking Time:45 Minutes
Ingredients:
- 1 tablespoon extra-virgin olive oil
- ½ teaspoon salt
- 1½ pounds carrots, peeled

Directions:
1. Cut parchment paper into 11-inch circle, then cut 1-inch hole in center, folding paper as needed.
2. Bring 3 cups water, oil, and salt to simmer in 12-inch skillet over high heat. Off heat, add carrots, top with parchment, cover skillet, and let sit for 20 minutes.
3. Uncover, leaving parchment in place, and bring to simmer over high heat. Reduce heat to medium-low and cook until most of water has evaporated and carrots are very tender, about 45 minutes.
4. Discard parchment, increase heat to medium-high, and cook, shaking skillet often, until carrots are lightly glazed and no water remains, 2 to 4 minutes. Serve.

Nutrition Info:
- 60 cal., 2g fat (0g sag. fat), 0mg chol, 100mg sod., 10g carb (5g sugars, 3g fiber), 1g pro.

Pan-roasted Broccoli

Servings:6
Cooking Time:10minutes
Ingredients:
- ¼ teaspoon salt
- ⅛ teaspoon pepper
- 2 tablespoons extra-virgin olive oil
- 1¾ pounds broccoli, florets cut into 1½-inch pieces, stalks peeled and cut on bias into ¼-inch-thick slices

Directions:
1. Stir 3 tablespoons water, salt, and pepper together in small bowl until salt dissolves; set aside. Heat oil in 12-inch nonstick skillet over medium-high heat until just smoking. Add broccoli stalks in even layer and cook, without stirring, until browned on bottoms, about 2 minutes. Add florets to skillet and toss to combine. Cook, without stirring, until bottoms of florets just begin to brown, 1 to 2 minutes.
2. Add water mixture and cover skillet. Cook until broccoli is bright green but still crisp, about 2 minutes. Uncover and continue to cook until water has evaporated, broccoli stalks are tender, and florets are crisp-tender, about 2 minutes. Serve.

Nutrition Info:
- 70 cal., 5g fat (0g sag. fat), 0mg chol, 125mg sod., 5g carb (1g sugars, 2g fiber), 2g pro.

Asparagus With Sesame Seeds

Servings: 2
Cooking Time: 15 Minutes
Ingredients:

- 1/2 pound fresh asparagus, trimmed
- 2 tablespoons water
- 1 teaspoon reduced-sodium soy sauce
- 1 teaspoon olive oil
- 1/8 teaspoon salt
- Dash pepper
- 1 teaspoon sesame seeds, toasted

Directions:

1. Place the asparagus in a steamer basket; place in a saucepan over 1 in. of water. Bring to a boil; cover and steam for 4-5 minutes or until crisp-tender. Transfer to a serving dish. Combine the water, soy sauce, oil, salt and pepper; drizzle over asparagus. Sprinkle with sesame seeds.

Nutrition Info:

- 43 cal., 3 g fat (trace sat. fat), 0 chol., 262 mg sodium, 3 g carb., 1 g fiber, 2 g pro.

Boiled Carrots With Paprika And Mint

Servings:4
Cooking Time:x
Ingredients:

- 1 pound carrots, peeled
- Salt
- 1 tablespoon extra-virgin olive oil
- 1 teaspoon sherry vinegar, plus extra for serving
- ½ teaspoon paprika
- 1 tablespoon chopped fresh mint

Directions:

1. Cut carrots into 1½- to 2-inch lengths. Leave thin pieces whole, halve medium pieces lengthwise, and quarter thick pieces lengthwise.
2. Bring 2 cups water to boil in medium saucepan over high heat. Add carrots and ⅛ teaspoon salt, cover, and cook until tender throughout, about 6 minutes (start timer as soon as carrots go into water).
3. Drain carrots and return them to now-empty saucepan. Add oil, vinegar, paprika, and pinch salt and stir until combined. Stir in mint. Season with extra vinegar to taste. Serve.

Nutrition Info:

- 70 cal., 4g fat (0g sag. fat), 0mg chol, 140mg sod., 10g carb (5g sugars, 3g fiber), 1g pro.

Easy Baked Mushrooms

Servings: 4
Cooking Time: 30 Minutes
Ingredients:
- 1 pound medium fresh mushrooms, halved
- 2 tablespoons olive oil
- 1/4 cup seasoned bread crumbs
- 1/4 teaspoon garlic powder
- 1/4 teaspoon pepper
- Fresh parsley, optional

Directions:
1. Place mushrooms on a baking sheet. Drizzle with oil; toss to coat. In a small bowl, combine the bread crumbs, garlic powder and pepper; sprinkle over the mushrooms.
2. Bake, uncovered, at 425° for 18-20 minutes or until lightly browned. Garnish with parsley if desired.

Nutrition Info:
- 116 cal., 8 g fat (1 g sat. fat), 0 chol., 112 mg sodium, 10 g carb., 2 g fiber, 4 g pro.

Pesto Pasta & Potatoes

Servings:12
Cooking Time: 30 Minutes
Ingredients:
- 1 1/2 pounds small red potatoes, halved
- 12 ounces uncooked whole grain spiral pasta
- 3 cups cut fresh or frozen green beans
- 1 jar (6 1/2 ounces) prepared pesto
- 1 cup grated Parmigiano-Reggiano cheese

Directions:
1. Place potatoes in a large saucepan; add water to cover. Bring to a boil. Reduce heat; cook, uncovered, until tender, 8-10 minutes. Drain; transfer to a large bowl.
2. Meanwhile, cook pasta according to package directions, adding green beans during the last 5 minutes of cooking. Drain, reserving 3/4 cup pasta water, and add to potatoes. Toss with the pesto, cheese blend and enough pasta water to moisten.

Nutrition Info:
- 261 cal., 10g fat (3g sat. fat), 11mg chol., 233mg sod., 34g carb. (2g sugars, 5g fiber), 11g pro.

Hot Skillet Pineapple

Servings: 4
Cooking Time: 7 Minutes

Ingredients:
- 2 tablespoons no-trans-fat margarine (35% vegetable oil)
- 1 1/2 teaspoons packed dark brown sugar
- 1/2 teaspoon ground curry powder
- 8 slices pineapple packed in juice

Directions:
1. Place a large nonstick skillet over medium-high heat until hot. Add the margarine, sugar, and curry and bring to a boil. Stir to blend.
2. Arrange the pineapple slices in a single layer in the skillet. Cook 6 minutes until the pineapples are richly golden in color, turning frequently.
3. Arrange the pineapples on a serving platter and let stand 5 minutes to develop flavors and cool slightly. Serve hot or room temperature.

Nutrition Info:
- 70 cal., 2g fat (0g sag. fat), 0mg chol, 45mg sod., 13g carb (12g sugars, 1g fiber), 0g pro.

Spicy Green Beans With Caramelized Onions

Servings: 8
Cooking Time: 25 Minutes

Ingredients:
- 1 tablespoon olive oil
- 1 tablespoon sugar
- 1 large white onion, thinly sliced (1½ cups)
- 1 lb fresh green beans, trimmed
- 2 tablespoons reduced-sodium soy sauce
- ½ teaspoon salt
- ½ teaspoon crushed red pepper flakes

Directions:
1. In 10-inch skillet, heat oil and sugar over medium heat, stirring occasionally. Add onion; cook 10 to 15 minutes, stirring frequently, until tender and light golden brown. Remove onion from skillet.
2. To same skillet, add remaining ingredients. Cook 3 to 5 minutes, stirring constantly, until beans are crisp-tender. Stir in onion; cook until thoroughly heated.

Nutrition Info:
- 50 cal., 2g fat (0g sat. fat), 0 chol., 280mg sod., 8g carb. (4g sugars, 2g fiber), 1g pro.

Saucy Eggplant And Capers

Servings: 4
Cooking Time:21 Minutes
Ingredients:
- 10 ounces eggplant, diced (about 2 1/2 cups)
- 1 (14.5-ounce) can stewed tomatoes with Italian seasonings
- 2 tablespoons chopped fresh basil
- 2 teaspoons capers, drained
- 2 teaspoons extra virgin olive oil (optional)

Directions:
1. Bring the eggplant and tomatoes to boil in a large saucepan over high heat. Reduce the heat, cover tightly, and simmer 20 minutes or until the eggplant is very tender.
2. Remove the saucepan from the heat, stir in the basil, capers, and 2 teaspoons extra virgin olive oil (if desired), and let stand 3 minutes to develop flavors.

Nutrition Info:
- 50 cal., 0g fat (0g sag. fat), 0mg chol, 250mg sod., 12g carb (7g sugars, 3g fiber), 2g pro.

Roasted Cauliflower

Servings:6
Cooking Time:20 Minutes
Ingredients:
- 1 head cauliflower (2 pounds)
- ¼ cup extra-virgin olive oil
- Salt and pepper

Directions:
1. Adjust oven rack to lowest position and heat oven to 475 degrees. Line a rimmed baking sheet with aluminum foil. Trim outer leaves off cauliflower and cut stem flush with bottom of head. Cut head into 8 equal wedges. Place wedges, with either cut side down, on lined baking sheet, drizzle with 2 tablespoons oil, and sprinkle with ¼ teaspoon salt and ⅛ teaspoon pepper. Gently rub oil and seasonings into cauliflower. Gently flip cauliflower and repeat on second cut side with remaining 2 tablespoons oil, ¼ teaspoon salt, and ⅛ teaspoon pepper.
2. Cover baking sheet tightly with foil and roast for 10 minutes. Remove foil and continue to roast until bottoms of cauliflower wedges are golden, 8 to 12 minutes.
3. Remove sheet from oven, carefully flip wedges using spatula, and continue to roast until cauliflower is golden all over, 8 to 12 minutes. Transfer to serving dish, season with pepper to taste, and serve.

Nutrition Info:
- 120 cal., 10g fat (1g sag. fat), 0mg chol, 240mg sod., 8g carb (3g sugars, 3g fiber), 3g pro.

Roasted Broccoli

Servings:6
Cooking Time:x
Ingredients:
- 1¾ pounds broccoli
- 3 tablespoons extra-virgin olive oil
- 3 garlic cloves, minced
- ½ teaspoon salt
- Pinch pepper
- Lemon wedges

Directions:
1. Adjust oven rack to lowest position, place rimmed baking sheet on rack, and heat oven to 500 degrees. Cut broccoli horizontally at juncture of crowns and stalks. Cut crowns into 4 wedges (if 3 to 4 inches in diameter) or 6 wedges (if 4 to 5 inches in diameter). Trim tough outer peel from stalks, then cut into ½-inch-thick planks that are 2 to 3 inches long.
2. Combine oil, garlic, salt, and pepper in large bowl. Add broccoli and toss to coat. Working quickly, lay broccoli in single layer, flat sides down, on preheated sheet. Roast until stalks are well browned and tender and florets are lightly browned, 9 to 11 minutes. Transfer to serving dish and serve with lemon wedges.

Nutrition Info:
- 90 cal., 7g fat (1g sag. fat), 0mg chol, 220mg sod., 6g carb (1g sugars, 2g fiber), 2g pro.

Best Baked Sweet Potatoes

Servings:4
Cooking Time:8minutes
Ingredients:
- 4 (8-ounce) sweet potatoes, unpeeled, each lightly pricked with fork in 3 places

Directions:
1. Adjust oven rack to middle position and heat oven to 425 degrees. Place wire rack in aluminum foil–lined rimmed baking sheet and spray rack with vegetable oil spray. Place potatoes on large plate and microwave until potatoes yield to gentle pressure and reach internal temperature of 200 degrees, 6 to 9 minutes, flipping potatoes every 3 minutes.
2. Transfer potatoes to prepared rack and bake for 1 hour (exteriors of potatoes will be lightly browned and potatoes will feel very soft when squeezed).
3. Slit each potato lengthwise; using clean dish towel, hold ends and squeeze slightly to push flesh up and out. Transfer potatoes to serving dish. Serve.

Nutrition Info:
- 170 cal., 0g fat (0g sag. fat), 0mg chol, 120mg sod., 40g carb (12g sugars, 7g fiber), 3g pro.

Easy Sauteed Spinach

Servings: 4
Cooking Time: 20 Minutes
Ingredients:

- 1 small onion, finely chopped
- 1 garlic clove, minced
- 2 packages (6 ounces each) fresh baby spinach
- 3 tablespoons sherry or reduced-sodium chicken broth
- 1/4 teaspoon salt
- 1/8 teaspoon pepper
- 1 tablespoon pine nuts

Directions:

1. In a large nonstick skillet coated with cooking spray, saute onion until tender. Add garlic; cook 1 minute longer. Stir in the spinach, sherry, salt and pepper; cook and stir for 4-5 minutes or until the spinach is wilted. Sprinkle with the pine nuts.

Nutrition Info:

- 47 cal., 1 g fat (trace sat. fat), 0 chol., 216 mg sodium, 5 g carb., 2 g fiber, 3 g pro.

Sautéed Zucchini Ribbons

Servings:6
Cooking Time:x
Ingredients:

- 1 small garlic clove, minced
- 1 teaspoon grated lemon zest plus 1 tablespoon juice
- 4 (6- to 8-ounce) zucchini and/or yellow summer squash, trimmed
- 2 tablespoons plus 1 teaspoon extra-virgin olive oil
- Salt and pepper
- 1½ tablespoons chopped fresh parsley

Directions:

1. Combine garlic and lemon juice in large bowl and set aside for at least 10 minutes. Using vegetable peeler, shave off 3 ribbons from 1 side of summer squash, then turn squash 90 degrees and shave off 3 more ribbons. Continue to turn and shave ribbons until you reach seeds; discard core. Repeat with remaining squash.
2. Whisk 2 tablespoons oil, ¼ teaspoon salt, ⅛ teaspoon pepper, and lemon zest into garlic–lemon juice mixture.
3. Heat remaining 1 teaspoon oil in 12-inch nonstick skillet over medium-high heat until just smoking. Add squash and cook, tossing occasionally with tongs, until squash has softened and is translucent, 3 to 4 minutes. Transfer squash to bowl with dressing, add parsley, and gently toss to coat. Season with pepper to taste. Serve.

Nutrition Info:

- 70 cal., 6g fat (1g sag. fat), 0mg chol, 105mg sod., 4g carb (2g sugars, 1g fiber), 1g pro.

Buttery Tarragon Sugar Snaps

Servings: 4
Cooking Time:8 Minutes
Ingredients:

- 8 ounces sugar snap peas, trimmed
- 1 1/2 tablespoons no-trans-fat margarine (35% vegetable oil)
- 1 tablespoon chopped fresh parsley
- 1/2 teaspoon dried tarragon
- 1/4 teaspoon salt

Directions:

1. Steam the sugar snaps for 6 minutes or until they are tender-crisp.
2. Place them in a serving bowl, add the remaining ingredients, and toss gently.

Nutrition Info:

- 45 cal., 2g fat (0g sag. fat), 0mg chol, 180mg sod., 5g carb (2g sugars, 1g fiber), 1g pro.

Roasted Sesame Asparagus

Servings: 4
Cooking Time: 15 Minutes
Ingredients:

- 1 lb fresh asparagus spears (about 16)
- 1 tablespoon dark sesame oil
- 1 teaspoon soy sauce
- ½ teaspoon wasabi paste
- ¼ teaspoon black or white sesame seed

Directions:

1. Heat oven to 450°F. Break off tough ends of asparagus as far down as stalks snap easily. In ungreased 15 × 10 × 1-inch pan, place asparagus spears in single layer.
2. In small bowl, mix remaining ingredients except sesame seed; pour over asparagus, turning asparagus to coat evenly.
3. Roast 8 to 10 minutes or until asparagus is crisp-tender (asparagus will appear slightly charred). Sprinkle with sesame seed.

Nutrition Info:

- 50 cal., 3.5g fat (0.5g sat. fat), 0 chol., 75mg sod., 2g carb. (1g sugars, 1g fiber), 1g pro.

Fresh Lemon Roasted Brussels Sprouts

Servings: 4
Cooking Time:20 Minutes
Ingredients:

- 1 pound fresh Brussels sprouts, ends trimmed and halved
- 2 tablespoons extra-virgin olive oil, divided
- Juice and zest of 1 medium lemon
- 2 teaspoons Worcestershire sauce
- 1/4 teaspoon pepper

Directions:

1. Preheat oven 425°F.
2. Toss Brussels sprouts with 1 tablespoon oil, place in a single layer on a foil-lined baking sheet. Roast 10 minutes, stir, and cook 10 minutes or until just tender and beginning to brown.
3. Remove, toss with remaining ingredients and 1/4 teaspoon salt, if desired.

Nutrition Info:

- 115 cal., 7g fat (1g sag. fat), 0mg chol, 55mg sod., 13g carb (3g sugars, 5g fiber), 4g pro.

Herb-crusted Potatoes

Servings: 4
Cooking Time: 50 Minutes
Ingredients:
- 1 1/2 pounds Yukon Gold potatoes, cut into wedges
- 1 tablespoon olive oil
- 1 tablespoon minced fresh rosemary
- 1 teaspoon dried thyme
- 1 teaspoon dried oregano
- 1/2 teaspoon salt
- 1/4 to 1/2 teaspoon pepper

Directions:
1. In a large bowl, toss potatoes with oil. Combine the seasonings; sprinkle over potatoes and toss to coat.
2. Arrange in a single layer in a 15-in. x 10-in. x 1-in. baking pan coated with cooking spray. Bake at 425° for 40-45 minutes or until tender, stirring once.

Nutrition Info:
- 155 cal., 4 g fat (1 g sat. fat), 0 chol., 312 mg sodium, 27 g carb., 3 g fiber, 3 g pro.

Pimiento Brussels Sprouts

Servings: 4
Cooking Time: 15 Minutes
Ingredients:
- 1 package (16 ounces) frozen Brussels sprouts
- 4 1/2 teaspoons butter
- 4 1/2 teaspoons white vinegar
- 3/4 teaspoon dried tarragon
- 1/4 teaspoon salt
- 1 jar (2 ounces) diced pimientos, drained

Directions:
1. Cook Brussels sprouts according to package directions. Drain, reserving 1 tablespoon liquid; keep sprouts warm.
2. In a small saucepan, melt butter; stir in the vinegar, tarragon, salt and reserved cooking liquid. Pour over sprouts and toss to coat. Sprinkle with the pimientos.

Nutrition Info:
- 88 cal., 5 g fat (3 g sat. fat), 11 mg chol., 191 mg sodium, 10 g carb., 5 g fiber, 5 g pro.

Light Glazed Skillet Apples

Servings: 4
Cooking Time:5 Minutes
Ingredients:
- 1 tablespoon no-trans-fat margarine
- 1/2 tablespoon sugar
- 2 cups Granny Smith apple slices

Directions:
1. Melt the margarine in a large skillet over medium heat, then tilt the skillet to coat the bottom evenly. Sprinkle the sugar evenly over the skillet bottom.
2. Arrange the apples in a single layer on top of the sugar. Cook 1–1 1/2 minutes or until the apples just begin to turn golden. Do not stir.
3. Using two forks or a spoon and a fork for easy handling, turn the apple slices over and cook 1 minute. Continue to cook and turn again until the apples are golden on both sides, about 2 minutes longer.

Nutrition Info:
- 45 cal., 1g fat (0g sag. fat), 0mg chol, 20mg sod., 9g carb (7g sugars, 1g fiber), 0g pro.

Squash Melt

Servings: 4
Cooking Time:8 Minutes
Ingredients:
- 2 medium yellow squash (about 12 ounces total), cut in 1/8-inch rounds
- 1 medium green bell pepper, chopped or 1 cup thinly sliced yellow onion
- 1/4–1/2 teaspoon dried oregano
- 1/4 teaspoon salt
- 1/4 cup shredded, reduced-fat, sharp cheddar cheese

Directions:
1. Place a medium nonstick skillet over medium-high heat until hot. Coat the skillet with nonstick cooking spray and add all the ingredients except the cheese.
2. Coat the vegetables with nonstick cooking spray and cook 6–7 minutes or until the vegetables are tender, stirring constantly. Use two utensils to stir as you would when stir-frying.
3. Remove the skillet from the heat and sprinkle the vegetables evenly with the cheese. Cover and let stand 2 minutes to melt the cheese.

Nutrition Info:
- 40 cal., 1g fat (0g sag. fat), 5mg chol, 190mg sod., 5g carb (3g sugars, 2g fiber), 3g pro.

Roasted Beans And Green Onions

Servings: 4
Cooking Time:11 Minutes
Ingredients:

- 8 ounces green string beans, trimmed
- 4 whole green onions, trimmed and cut in fourths (about 3-inch pieces)
- 1 1/2 teaspoons extra virgin olive oil
- 1/4 teaspoon salt

Directions:

1. Preheat the oven to 425°F.
2. Line a baking sheet with foil and coat the foil with nonstick cooking spray.
3. Toss the beans, onions, and oil together in a medium bowl. Arrange them in a thin layer on the baking sheet.
4. Bake for 8 minutes and stir gently, using two utensils as you would for a stir-fry. Bake another 3–4 minutes or until the beans begin to brown on the edges and are tender-crisp.
5. Remove the pan from the oven and sprinkle the beans with salt.

Nutrition Info:

- 35 cal., 2g fat (0g sag. fat), 0mg chol, 150mg sod., 5g carb (1g sugars, 2g fiber), 1g pro.

Roasted Dijon Broccoli

Servings: 4
Cooking Time: 20 Minutes
Ingredients:

- 1 bunch broccoli, cut into florets
- 2 tablespoons olive oil
- 1 tablespoon red wine vinegar
- 1 teaspoon Dijon mustard
- 1 garlic clove, minced
- 1/4 teaspoon salt
- 1/4 teaspoon pepper

Directions:

1. Place broccoli on a baking sheet. In a small bowl, whisk the remaining ingredients. Drizzle over broccoli; toss to coat.
2. Bake, uncovered, at 425° for 10-15 minutes or until tender.

Nutrition Info:

- 106 cal., 7 g fat (1 g sat. fat), 0 chol., 219 mg sodium, 9 g carb., 5 g fiber, 5 g pro.

Dilly Spinach With Mushrooms

Servings: 2
Cooking Time: 15 Minutes
Ingredients:

- 2 teaspoons olive oil
- 1 clove garlic, finely chopped
- 1 cup sliced fresh mushrooms (3 oz)
- 1 bag (6 oz) washed fresh baby spinach leaves (about 7 cups)
- ¼ teaspoon salt
- ⅛ teaspoon dried dill weed
- 1 tablespoon pine nuts, toasted

Directions:

1. In 4-quart Dutch oven, heat oil over medium heat. Add garlic and mushrooms; cook about 3 minutes, stirring constantly, until mushrooms are crisp-tender.
2. Stir in spinach, salt and dill weed. Cook 3 to 4 minutes, stirring occasionally, until spinach is hot and wilted. Sprinkle with nuts.

Nutrition Info:

- 110 cal., 8g fat (1g sat. fat), 0 chol., 370mg sod., 6g carb. (1g sugars, 3g fiber), 4g pro.

Roasted Smashed Potatoes

Servings:6
Cooking Time:60 Minutes
Ingredients:

- 2 pounds small Red Bliss potatoes (about 18), scrubbed
- ¼ cup extra-virgin olive oil
- 1 teaspoon chopped fresh thyme
- 1 teaspoon kosher salt
- ⅛ teaspoon pepper

Directions:

1. Adjust oven racks to top and bottom positions and heat oven to 500 degrees. Arrange potatoes on rimmed baking sheet, pour ¾ cup water into baking sheet, and wrap tightly with aluminum foil. Cook on bottom rack until paring knife or skewer slips in and out of potatoes easily (poke through foil to test), 25 to 30 minutes. Remove foil and cool 10 minutes. If any water remains on baking sheet, blot dry with paper towel.
2. Drizzle 2 tablespoons oil over potatoes and roll to coat. Space potatoes evenly on baking sheet and place second baking sheet on top; press down firmly on baking sheet, flattening potatoes until ⅓ to ½ inch thick. Remove top sheet and sprinkle potatoes evenly with thyme, salt, and pepper. Drizzle evenly with remaining 2 tablespoons oil.
3. Roast potatoes on top rack for 15 minutes. Transfer potatoes to bottom rack and continue to roast until well browned, 20 to 30 minutes longer. Serve immediately.

Nutrition Info:

- 190 cal., 10g fat (1g sag. fat), 0mg chol, 210mg sod., 24g carb (2g sugars, 3g fiber), 3g pro.

Grilled Soy Pepper Petites

Servings: 4
Cooking Time:12 Minutes
Ingredients:

- 1 pound petite peppers
- 3 tablespoons apricot or raspberry fruit spread
- 1 1/2 tablespoons light soy sauce
- 1/8 to 1/4 teaspoon dried pepper flakes

Directions:
1. Heat a grill or grill pan over medium-high heat. Coat peppers with cooking spray and cook 12 minutes or until tender and beginning to char, turning frequently.
2. Meanwhile, heat fruit spread in microwave for 15 seconds to melt slightly; whisk in soy sauce and pepper flakes.
3. Place peppers in a shallow bowl or rimmed platter and toss with mixture. Serve warm or room temperature.

Nutrition Info:
- 55 cal., 0g fat (0g sag. fat), 0mg chol, 200mg sod., 12g carb (9g sugars, 2g fiber), 2g pro.

Crunchy Pear And Cilantro Relish

Servings: 4
Cooking Time: 6 Minutes
Ingredients:

- 2 firm medium pears, peeled, cored, and finely chopped (about 1/4-inch cubes)
- 3/4 teaspoon lime zest
- 3 tablespoons lime juice
- 1 1/4 tablespoons sugar
- 3 tablespoons chopped cilantro or mint

Directions:
1. Place all ingredients in a bowl and toss well.
2. Serve immediately for peak flavor and texture.

Nutrition Info:
- 50 cal., 0g fat (0g sag. fat), 0mg chol, 0mg sod., 14g carb (9g sugars, 3g fiber), 0g pro.

Skillet-roasted Veggies

Servings: 4
Cooking Time:6 Minutes
Ingredients:

- 5 ounces asparagus spears, trimmed and cut into 2-inch pieces (1 cup total), patted dry
- 3 ounces sliced portobello mushrooms (1/2 of a 6-ounce package)
- 1/2 medium red bell pepper, cut in thin strips
- 1/4 teaspoon salt
- 1/8 teaspoon black pepper

Directions:
1. Place a large nonstick skillet over medium-high heat until hot. Coat the skillet with nonstick cooking spray and add the asparagus, mushrooms, and bell pepper. Coat the vegetables with nonstick cooking spray and sprinkle evenly with the salt and black pepper.
2. Cook 5–6 minutes, or until the vegetables begin to richly brown on the edges. Use two utensils to stir as you would when stir-frying.
3. Remove from the heat, cover tightly, and let stand 2 minutes to develop flavors.

Nutrition Info:
- 15 cal., 0g fat (0g sag. fat), 0mg chol, 150mg sod., 3g carb (1g sugars, 1g fiber), 1g pro.

Broiled Eggplant With Basil

Servings:6
Cooking Time:9 Minutes
Ingredients:

- 1½ pounds eggplant, sliced into ¼-inch-thick rounds
- Kosher salt and pepper
- 3 tablespoons extra-virgin olive oil
- 2 tablespoons chopped fresh basil

Directions:
1. Spread eggplant on paper towel–lined baking sheet, sprinkle both sides with 1½ teaspoons salt, and let sit for 9 minutes.
2. Adjust oven rack 4 inches from broiler element and heat broiler. Thoroughly pat eggplant dry with paper towels, arrange on aluminum foil–lined rimmed baking sheet in single layer, and brush both sides with oil. Broil eggplant until mahogany brown and lightly charred, about 4 minutes per side. Transfer eggplant to serving platter, season with pepper to taste, and sprinkle with basil. Serve.

Nutrition Info:
- 90 cal., 7g fat (1g sag. fat), 0mg chol, 140mg sod., 7g carb (4g sugars, 3g fiber), 1g pro.

Roasted Spiralized Sweet Potatoes With Walnuts And Feta

Servings:6
Cooking Time:x
Ingredients:

- 2 pounds sweet potatoes, peeled
- 2 tablespoons extra-virgin olive oil
- Salt and pepper
- ¼ cup walnuts, toasted and chopped coarse
- 1 ounce feta cheese, crumbled (¼ cup)
- 2 tablespoons chopped fresh parsley

Directions:
1. Adjust oven rack to middle position and heat oven to 450 degrees. Using spiralizer, cut sweet potatoes into ⅛-inch-thick noodles, then cut noodles into 12-inch lengths.
2. Toss potato noodles with 1 tablespoon oil, ¼ teaspoon salt, and ⅛ teaspoon pepper and spread on rimmed baking sheet. Roast until potatoes are just tender, 12 to 14 minutes, stirring once halfway through roasting.
3. Season potatoes with pepper to taste and transfer to serving platter. Sprinkle walnuts, feta, and parsley over top, then drizzle with remaining 1 tablespoon oil. Serve.

Nutrition Info:
- 180 cal., 8g fat (1g sag. fat), 5mg chol, 210mg sod., 24g carb (7g sugars, 4g fiber), 3g pro.

Broccoli, Pepper And Bacon Toss

Servings: 6
Cooking Time: 15 Minutes
Ingredients:

- 6 cups frozen broccoli florets
- 2 cups frozen stir-fry bell peppers and onions (from 1-lb bag)
- ½ cup raisins
- 2 tablespoons reduced-fat coleslaw dressing
- 2 tablespoons real bacon pieces (from 2.8-oz package)

Directions:

1. Cook broccoli and stir-fry bell peppers and onions mixture separately in microwave as directed on packages. Drain well.
2. In large bowl, toss broccoli, bell pepper mixture, raisins and coleslaw dressing. Sprinkle with bacon. Serve warm.

Nutrition Info:

- 130 cal., 2g fat (0g sat. fat), 0 chol., 70mg sod., 22g carb. (12g sugars, 5g fiber), 6g pro.

Chapter 10. Vegetarian Recipes

"refried" Bean And Rice Casserole

Servings: 4
Cooking Time:15 Minutes
Ingredients:

- 2 1/4 cups cooked brown rice (omit added salt or fat)
- 1 (15.5-ounce) can dark red kidney beans, rinsed and drained
- 7 tablespoons picante sauce
- 1/4 cup water
- 1/2 cup shredded, reduced-fat, sharp cheddar cheese

Directions:

1. Preheat the oven to 350°F.
2. Coat an 8-inch-square baking pan with nonstick cooking spray. Place the rice in the pan and set aside.
3. Add the beans, picante sauce, and water to a blender and blend until pureed, scraping the sides of the blender frequently.
4. Spread the bean mixture evenly over the rice and sprinkle with cheese. Bake, uncovered, for 15 minutes or until thoroughly heated.

Nutrition Info:

- 260 cal., 3g fat (1g sag. fat), 5mg chol, 430mg sod., 44g carb (1g sugars, 7g fiber), 14g pro.

Hurried Hummus Wraps

Servings: 4
Cooking Time: 5 Minutes
Ingredients:
- 4 whole-wheat flour tortillas
- 1/2 cup prepared hummus
- 6 cups packed mixed greens or spring greens
- 2 ounces crumbled reduced-fat feta or reduced-fat bleu cheese

Directions:
1. Warm tortillas according to package directions.
2. Top each with 2 tablespoons hummus, 1 1/2 cups lettuce, and 2 tablespoons cheese, roll tightly and cut in half.

Nutrition Info:
- 210 cal., 14g fat (2g sag. fat), 5mg chol, 420mg sod., 28g carb (1g sugars, 4g fiber), 8g pro.

Speedy Greek Orzo Salad

Servings: 9
Cooking Time:7 Minutes
Ingredients:
- 8 ounces uncooked whole-wheat orzo pasta
- 1/2 cup reduced-fat olive oil vinaigrette salad dressing (divided use)
- 3 tablespoons salt-free Greek seasoning (sold in jars in the spice aisle)
- 2 ounces crumbled, reduced-fat, sun-dried tomato and basil feta cheese
- 2 tablespoons chopped fresh parsley (optional)

Directions:
1. Cook the pasta according to package directions, omitting any salt and fat.
2. Meanwhile, stir 1/4 cup salad dressing and the Greek seasoning together in a medium bowl.
3. Drain the pasta in a colander and run under cold water until cooled. Shake off excess liquid and add it to the salad dressing mixture. Toss well, then add the feta and toss gently. Cover the bowl with plastic wrap and refrigerate at least 1 hour.
4. At serving time, add 1/4 cup salad dressing and toss to coat. Sprinkle with 2 tablespoons chopped fresh parsley, if desired.

Nutrition Info:
- 130 cal., 4g fat (1g sag. fat), 5mg chol, 180mg sod., 20g carb (1g sugars, 5g fiber), 4g pro.

Iced Tea Parfaits

Servings: 4
Cooking Time: 15 Minutes
Ingredients:

- 2 cups water
- 3 individual tea bags
- 1 package (3 ounces) lemon gelatin
- 4 maraschino cherries
- 1 1/2 cups whipped topping, divided
- 4 lemon slices

Directions:

1. In a small saucepan, bring the water to a boil. Remove from the heat; add tea bags. Cover and steep for 5 minutes. Discard the tea bags. Stir the gelatin into tea until completely dissolved. Cool slightly.
2. Pour 1/4 cup gelatin mixture into each of four parfait glasses. Place a cherry in each glass; refrigerate until set but not firm, about 1 hour. Transfer remaining gelatin mixture to a small bowl; refrigerate for 1 hour or until soft-set.
3. Whisk reserved gelatin mixture for 2-3 minutes or until smooth. Stir in 1/2 cup whipped topping; spoon into parfait glasses. Refrigerate for at least 2 hours. Just before serving, top with remaining whipped topping and garnish with lemon slices.

Nutrition Info:

- 162 cal., 5 g fat (5 g sat. fat), 0 chol., 48 mg sodium, 27 g carb., 0 fiber, 2 g pro.

Tomato Topper Over Anything

Servings: 3
Cooking Time:22 Minutes
Ingredients:

- 1 (14.5-ounce) can no-salt-added tomatoes with green pepper and onion
- 1/2 cup chopped roasted red peppers
- 2–3 tablespoons chopped fresh basil
- 2 teaspoons extra virgin olive oil

Directions:

1. Bring the tomatoes and peppers to boil in a medium saucepan. Reduce the heat and simmer, uncovered, for 15 minutes or until slightly thickened, stirring occasionally.
2. Remove the mixture from the heat, stir in the basil and oil, and let stand 5 minutes to develop flavors.

Nutrition Info:

- 80 cal., 3g fat (0g sag. fat), 0mg chol, 90mg sod., 12g carb (8g sugars, 2g fiber), 2g pro.

Black Bean And Corn Bowl

Servings: 4
Cooking Time:22 Minutes
Ingredients:

- 1 (10.5-ounce) can mild tomatoes with green chilis
- 1 (15-ounce) can black beans, rinsed and drained
- 2 cups frozen corn kernels
- 1/4 cup reduced-fat sour cream

Directions:

1. Place all ingredients except the sour cream in a large saucepan. Bring to a boil over high heat, then reduce the heat, cover, and simmer 20 minutes.
2. Serve in 4 individual bowls topped with 1 tablespoon sour cream.

Nutrition Info:

- 170 cal., 2g fat (1g sag. fat), 5mg chol, 310mg sod., 31g carb (6g sugars, 7g fiber), 9g pro.

Apricot Gelatin Mold

Servings: 12
Cooking Time: 35 Minutes
Ingredients:

- 1 can (8 ounces) unsweetened crushed pineapple
- 2 packages (3 ounces each) apricot or peach gelatin
- 1 package (8 ounces) reduced-fat cream cheese
- 3/4 cup grated carrots
- 1 carton (8 ounces) frozen fat-free whipped topping, thawed

Directions:

1. Drain pineapple, reserving juice in a 2-cup measuring cup; add enough water to measure 2 cups. Set pineapple aside. Pour juice mixture into a small saucepan. Bring to a boil; remove from heat. Dissolve gelatin in juice mixture. Cool for 10 minutes.
2. In a large bowl, beat cream cheese until creamy. Gradually add gelatin mixture, beating until smooth. Refrigerate for 30-40 minutes or until slightly thickened.
3. Fold in pineapple and carrots, then whipped topping. Transfer to an 8-cup ring mold coated with cooking spray. Refrigerate until set. Unmold onto a serving platter.

Nutrition Info:

- 144 cal., 4 g fat (3 g sat. fat), 13 mg chol., 128 mg sodium, 23 g carb., trace fiber, 3 g pro.

Chocolate Peanut Butter Parfaits

Servings: 6
Cooking Time: 20 Minutes
Ingredients:

- 2 tablespoons reduced-fat chunky peanut butter
- 2 tablespoons plus 2 cups cold fat-free milk, divided
- 1 cup plus 6 tablespoons reduced-fat whipped topping, divided
- 1 package (1.4 ounces) sugar-free instant chocolate fudge pudding mix
- 3 tablespoons finely chopped salted peanuts

Directions:

1. In a small bowl, combine peanut butter and 2 tablespoons milk. Fold in 1 cup whipped topping; set aside. In another small bowl, whisk remaining milk with pudding mix for 2 minutes. Let stand for 2 minutes or until soft-set.
2. Spoon half of the pudding into six parfait glasses or dessert dishes. Layer with reserved peanut butter mixture and remaining pudding. Refrigerate for at least 1 hour. Refrigerate remaining whipped topping.
3. Just before serving, garnish each parfait with 1 tablespoon whipped topping and 1 1/2 teaspoons peanuts.

Nutrition Info:

- 146 cal., 6 g fat (3 g sat. fat), 2 mg chol., 300 mg sodium, 16 g carb., 1 g fiber, 6 g pro.

Cauliflower Steaks With Chimichurri Sauce

Servings:4
Cooking Time: 10 Minutes
Ingredients:

- 2 heads cauliflower (2 pounds each)
- ¼ cup extra-virgin olive oil
- Salt and pepper
- 1 recipe Chimichurri (this page)
- Lemon wedges

Directions:

1. Adjust oven rack to lowest position and heat oven to 500 degrees. Working with 1 head cauliflower at a time, discard outer leaves and trim stem flush with bottom florets. Halve cauliflower lengthwise through core. Cut one 1½-inch-thick slab lengthwise from each half, trimming any florets not connected to core. Repeat with remaining cauliflower. (You should have 4 steaks; reserve remaining cauliflower for another use.)
2. Place steaks on rimmed baking sheet and drizzle with 2 tablespoons oil. Sprinkle with pinch salt and ⅛ teaspoon pepper and rub to distribute. Flip steaks and repeat.
3. Cover sheet tightly with foil and roast for 5 minutes. Remove foil and continue to roast until bottoms of steaks are well browned, 8 to 10 minutes. Gently flip and continue to roast until cauliflower is tender and second sides are well browned, 6 to 8 minutes.
4. Transfer steaks to serving platter and brush tops evenly with ¼ cup chimichurri. Serve with lemon wedges and remaining chimichurri.

Nutrition Info:

- 370 cal., 29g fat (4g sag. fat), 0mg chol, 300mg sod., 24g carb (9g sugars, 10g fiber), 9g pro.

Mint Berry Blast

Servings: 4
Cooking Time: 10 Minutes
Ingredients:

- 1 cup each fresh raspberries, blackberries, blueberries and halved strawberries
- 1 tablespoon minced fresh mint
- 1 tablespoon lemon juice
- Whipped topping, optional

Directions:

1. In a large bowl, combine the berries, mint and lemon juice; gently toss to coat. Cover and refrigerate until serving. Garnish with whipped topping if desired.

Nutrition Info:

- 65 cal., 1 g fat (trace sat. fat), 0 chol., 1 mg sodium, 16 g carb., 6 g fiber, 1 g pro.

Pesto Potatoes And Edamame Bake

Servings: 4
Cooking Time:1 Hour
Ingredients:

- 1 1/2 pounds red potatoes, cut into 1/4-inch-thick slices
- 1 cup fresh or frozen, thawed shelled edamame
- 1/2 cup prepared basil pesto
- 1/4 cup salted hulled pumpkin seeds

Directions:

1. Preheat oven to 350°F.
2. Coat a 2-quart baking dish with cooking spray. Arrange half of the potatoes on bottom of baking dish, overlapping slightly. Spoon half of the pesto evenly over all, top with the edamame, sprinkle with 1/4 teaspoon pepper. Repeat with remaining potatoes and pesto.
3. Cover and bake 55 minutes or until tender. Sprinkle with pumpkin seeds and bake, uncovered, 5 minutes.

Nutrition Info:

- 370 cal., 22g fat (3g sag. fat), 5mg chol, 380mg sod., 33g carb (3g sugars, 2g fiber), 14g pro.

Light Chocolate Truffles

Servings: 6
Cooking Time: 25 Minutes
Ingredients:

- 1/3 cup semisweet chocolate chips
- 4 ounces reduced-fat cream cheese
- 1/3 cup plus 2 teaspoons baking cocoa, divided
- 1 1/4 cups plus 2 teaspoons confectioners' sugar, divided

Directions:

1. In a microwave, melt chocolate chips; stir until smooth. Set aside.
2. In a small bowl, beat cream cheese until fluffy. Beat in 1/3 cup cocoa and melted chocolate. Gradually beat in 1 1/4 cups confectioners' sugar. Lightly coat hands with confectioners' sugar; roll chocolate mixture into 1-in. balls. Roll in the remaining cocoa or confectioners' sugar. Cover and refrigerate for at least 1 hour.

Nutrition Info:

- 62 cal., 2 g fat (1 g sat. fat), 4 mg chol., 24 mg sodium, 11 g carb., trace fiber, 1 g pro.

Low-fat Key Lime Pie

Servings: 8
Cooking Time: 20 Minutes
Ingredients:

- 1 package (.3 ounce) sugar-free lime gelatin
- 1/4 cup boiling water
- 2 cartons (6 ounces each) Key lime yogurt
- 1 carton (8 ounces) frozen fat-free whipped topping, thawed
- 1 reduced-fat graham cracker crust (8 inches)

Directions:
1. In a large bowl, dissolve gelatin in boiling water. Whisk in yogurt. Fold in whipped topping. Pour into crust.
2. Cover and refrigerate for at least 2 hours or until set.

Nutrition Info:
- 194 cal., 3 g fat (1 g sat. fat), 2 mg chol., 159 mg sodium, 33 g carb., 0 fiber, 3 g pro.

Skillet-grilled Meatless Burgers With Spicy Sour Cream

Servings: 4
Cooking Time:15 Minutes
Ingredients:

- 4 soy protein burgers (preferably the grilled variety)
- 1 1/2 cups thinly sliced onions
- 1/8 teaspoon salt (divided use)
- 1/4 cup fat-free sour cream
- 4–6 drops chipotle-flavored hot sauce

Directions:
1. Place a large nonstick skillet over medium heat until hot. Coat the skillet with nonstick cooking spray, add the patties, and cook 4 minutes on each side. Set the patties aside on a separate plate and cover with foil to keep warm.
2. Coat the skillet with nonstick cooking spray and increase the heat to medium high. Add the onions and 1/16 teaspoon salt. Lightly coat the onions with nonstick cooking spray and cook 5 minutes or until they are richly browned, stirring frequently.
3. Meanwhile, stir the sour cream, hot sauce, and 1/16 teaspoon salt together in a small bowl.
4. When the onions are browned, push them to one side of the skillet and add the patties. Spoon the onions on top of the patties and cook 1–2 minutes longer to heat thoroughly. Top each patty with 1 tablespoon sour cream.

Nutrition Info:
- 120 cal., 2g fat (0g sag. fat), 5mg chol, 440mg sod., 12g carb (2g sugars, 7g fiber), 16g pro.

Feta Basil Pasta

Servings: 4
Cooking Time:15 Minutes
Ingredients:
- 6 ounces whole-grain spaghetti, broken in half
- 4 ounces crumbled reduced-fat feta cheese
- 1/2 cup chopped fresh basil
- 1 cup grape tomatoes, quartered

Directions:
1. Cook pasta according to package directions, and drain.
2. Place pasta in a shallow bowl or rimmed platter. Top with the remaining ingredients in the order listed and sprinkle with 1/8 teaspoon salt and 1/8 teaspoon pepper, if desired.

Nutrition Info:
- 200 cal., 2g fat (0g sag. fat), 5mg chol, 250mg sod., 34g carb (1g sugars, 1g fiber), 14g pro.

Frozen Peach Yogurt

Servings: 6
Cooking Time: 20 Minutes
Ingredients:
- 4 medium peaches, peeled and sliced
- 1 envelope unflavored gelatin
- 1 cup fat-free milk
- 1/2 cup sugar
- Dash salt
- 2 1/2 cups vanilla yogurt
- 2 teaspoons vanilla extract

Directions:
1. Place peaches in a blender. Cover and process until blended; set aside. In a small saucepan, sprinkle gelatin over milk; let stand for 1 minute. Heat over low heat, stirring until the gelatin is completely dissolved. Remove from the heat; stir in sugar and salt until sugar dissolves. Add the yogurt, vanilla and reserved peaches.
2. Fill cylinder of ice cream freezer two-thirds full; freeze according to the manufacturer's directions. When yogurt is frozen, transfer to a freezer container; freeze for 2-4 hours before serving.

Nutrition Info:
- 149 cal., 1 g fat (1 g sat. fat), 4 mg chol., 83 mg sodium, 29 g carb., 1 g fiber, 6 g pro.

Toasted Grain And Arugula

Servings: 4
Cooking Time:20 Minutes
Ingredients:

- 4 ounces slivered almonds
- 1 cup dry bulgur
- 4 cups arugula
- 1/2 cup lite balsamic salad dressing

Directions:

1. Heat a large skillet over medium-high heat. Add the almonds and cook 2 minutes or until beginning to lightly brown, stirring constantly. Set aside on separate plate.
2. Add the bulgur to the skillet and cook (in the dry skillet) 3 minutes or until beginning to lightly brown, stirring constantly. Add 2 cups water, bring to a boil, reduce heat to low, cover, and simmer 12 minutes or until liquid is absorbed.
3. Remove from heat, place in a bowl with the arugula, 1/8 teaspoon salt, and 1/8 teaspoon pepper, if desired. Toss until arugula is slightly wilted.
4. Add the dressing to the skillet. Bring to a boil over medium-high heat and cook 2 minutes or until reduced to 1/3 cup. Immediately pour over the bulgur mixture and toss until well blended.

Nutrition Info:

- 310 cal., 16g fat (1g sag. fat), 0mg chol, 380mg sod., 39g carb (3g sugars, 10g fiber), 11g pro.

Open-faced Grilled Pepper-goat Cheese Sandwiches

Servings: 4
Cooking Time:25 Minutes
Ingredients:

- 3 large red bell peppers, halved lengthwise
- 1 1/2 tablespoons balsamic vinegar
- 8 ounces whole grain loaf bread, cut in half lengthwise
- 2 ounces crumbled goat cheese

Directions:

1. Heat grill or grill pan over medium-high heat. Flatten pepper halves with palm of hand. Coat both sides with cooking spray and cook 20 minutes or until tender, turning frequently. Place on cutting board and coarsely chop. Combine the peppers with the vinegar and 1/8 teaspoon salt, if desired. Cover to keep warm.
2. Coat both sides of the bread with cooking spray and cook 1 1/2 to 2 minutes on each side or until lightly browned. Cut each bread half crosswise into 4 pieces.
3. Top each bread slice with 1/4 cup pepper mixture and sprinkle cheese evenly over all.

Nutrition Info:

- 250 cal., 7g fat (3g sag. fat), 10mg chol, 280mg sod., 33g carb (10g sugars, 7g fiber), 12g pro.

Simple Lemon Pie

Servings: 8
Cooking Time: 20 Minutes
Ingredients:

- 1 package (.8 ounce) sugar-free cook-and-serve vanilla pudding mix
- 1 package (.3 ounce) sugar-free lemon gelatin
- 2 1/3 cups water
- 1/3 cup lemon juice
- 1 reduced-fat graham cracker crust (8 inches)
- 1 1/2 cups reduced-fat whipped topping

Directions:
1. In a small saucepan, combine pudding mix and gelatin. Add water and lemon juice; stir until smooth. Cook and stir over medium heat until mixture comes to a boil. Cook and stir 1-2 minutes longer or until thickened.
2. Remove from the heat; cool slightly. Pour into crust. Cover and refrigerate for 6 hours or overnight. Spread with whipped topping.

Nutrition Info:
- 146 cal., 5 g fat (3 g sat. fat), 0 chol., 174 mg sodium, 22 g carb., trace fiber, 2 g pro.

Cheesy Tortilla Rounds

Servings: 4
Cooking Time:14 Minutes
Ingredients:

- 4 (6-inch) soft corn tortillas
- 1 cup fat-free refried beans
- 1/2 cup shredded, reduced-fat mozzarella cheese
- 1 poblano chili pepper, seeded and thinly sliced, or 2 jalapeño chili peppers, seeded and thinly sliced

Directions:
1. Preheat the broiler.
2. Place a large nonstick skillet over medium-high heat until hot. Coat the skillet with nonstick cooking spray. Place two tortillas in the skillet and cook 1 minute or until they begin to lightly brown on the bottom. Turn them and cook 1 minute, then place on a baking sheet. Repeat with the other two tortillas.
3. Return the skillet to medium-high heat, coat with nonstick cooking spray, and add the peppers. Coat the peppers with nonstick cooking spray and cook 6 minutes or until they are tender and brown, stirring frequently. Remove them from the heat.
4. Spread equal amounts of beans evenly on each tortilla. Broil 4 inches away from the heat source for 1 minute. Sprinkle the cheese and pepper slices evenly over each tortilla and broil another 2 minutes or until the cheese has melted. Serve with lime wedges, if desired.

Nutrition Info:
- 150 cal., 3g fat (1g sag. fat), 10mg chol, 370mg sod., 23g carb (2g sugars, 5g fiber), 9g pro.

21 day meal plan

Day 1

Breakfast: Sweet Onion Frittata With Ham 16

Lunch: Anytime Skillet Pork 47

Dinner: Lemony Asparagus Spear Salad 91

Day 2

Breakfast: Fruity Cereal Bars 16

Lunch: Grapefruit-zested Pork 48

Dinner: Creamy Dill Cucumbers 92

Day 3

Breakfast: Honey Wheat Breadsticks 17t

Lunch: Cheesy Steak And Potato Skillet 48

Dinner: White Bean, Herb And Tomato Salad 92

Day 4

Breakfast: Spinach And Feta Omelets 17

Lunch: Southwestern Protein-powered Bowls 49

Dinner: Lemon Vinaigrette 92

Day 5

Breakfast: Morning Cinnamon Rolls 18

Lunch: Steak Marsala 50

Dinner: Toasted Pecan And Apple Salad 93

Day 6

Breakfast: Quick Veggie Frittata 18

Lunch: Prosciutto-pepper Pork Chops 50

Dinner: Feta'd Tuna With Greens 93

Day 7

Breakfast: Scrambled Eggs With Herbs 19

Lunch: Spicy Chili'd Sirloin Steak 51

Dinner: Ginger'd Ambrosia 94

Day 8

Breakfast: Good Morning Power Parfait 19

Lunch: Black Bean And Beef Tostadas 51

Dinner: Sausage Spinach Salad 94

Day 9

Breakfast: Cheesy Mushroom Omelet 20

Lunch: Christmas Carol Ham 51

Dinner: Artichoke Tomato Toss 95

Day 10

Breakfast: Orange-honey Yogurt 20

Lunch: Maple Pork With Figs 52

Dinner: Thousand Isle Wedges 95

Day 11

Breakfast: Sausage Potato Skillet Casserole 21

Lunch: Mediterranean Pasta Caesar Toss 52

Dinner: Caesar'd Chicken Salad 95

Day 12

Breakfast: Blackberry Smoothies 21

Lunch: Simple Teriyaki Steak Dinner 53

Dinner: Seaside Shrimp Salad 96

Day 13

Breakfast: Double-duty Banana Pancakes 22

Lunch: Chili-stuffed Potatoes 53

Dinner: Balsamic Bean Salsa Salad 96

Day 14

Breakfast: Yogurt Parfaits 22

Lunch: Chili Pork Tenderloin 54

Dinner: Bacon Onion Potato Salad 97

Day 15

Breakfast: Almond Quinoa With Cranberries 23

Lunch: Grilled Rosemary Lamb Chops 54

Dinner: Crispy Crunch Coleslaw 97

Day 16

Breakfast: Breakfast Grilled Swiss Cheese And Rye 23

Lunch: Sriracha-roasted Pork With Sweet Potatoes 55

Dinner: Pork And Avocado Salad 98

Day 17

Breakfast: Busy Day Breakfast Burrito 24

Lunch: Roasted Leg Of Lamb 55

Dinner: Pear And Bleu Cheese Greens 98

Day 18

Breakfast: English Muffin Melts 24

Lunch: Smoky Sirloin 56

Dinner: Cumin'd Salsa Salad 99

INDEX

136

Spiced Coffee 33

Spicy Chili'd Sirloin Steak 51

Spicy Green Beans With Caramelized Onions 114

Spinach And Feta Omelets 17

Squash Melt 120

Sriracha-roasted Pork With Sweet Potatoes 55

Steak Marsala 50

Strawberries With Balsamic Vinegar 88

Strawberry Breakfast Shortcakes 36

Strawberry Mousse 87

Strawberry Orange Vinegar 46

Strawberry Tofu Smoothies 31

Strawberry-carrot Smoothies 25

Strawberry-watermelon-pomegranate Smoothies 45

Sweet Jerk Pork 58

Sweet Onion Frittata With Ham 16

Sweet Peanut Buttery Dip 33

Sweet Pineapple Cider 38

Sweet Sherry'd Pork Tenderloin 64

T

Taco Chicken Tenders 73

Tangy Sweet Carrot Pepper Salad 100

Teriyaki Salmon 80

Thousand Isle Wedges 95

Toasted Grain And Arugula 133

Toasted Pecan And Apple Salad 93

Tomato Topper Over Anything 127

Tomato-jalapeno Granita 32

Tortellini Appetizers 30

Tropical Treats 28

Tuna Salad Stuffed Eggs 41

Turkey & Apricot Wraps 70

Turkey Patties With Dark Onion Gravy 73

Turkey Reubens 33

Turkey With Cranberry Sauce 72

Two-sauce Cajun Fish 82

W

Warm Figs With Goat Cheese And Honey 90

Weeknight Skillet Roast Chicken 69

Whipped Cauliflower 109

White Bean, Herb And Tomato Salad 92

Whole Wheat Buttermilk Rolls 26

Y

Yogurt Parfaits 22

Z

Zesty Beef Patties With Grilled Onions 49

Zesty Citrus Melon 101

Zippy Tortilla Chips 30

Made in the USA
Las Vegas, NV
07 November 2022

58921540R00077